I have many regrets in my life, but if I had read Robin Bertram's book *No Regrets* as a young man, things might be different. This is a manual for living your life to the fullest. It's about not looking back and wondering what might have been. If you've ever believed there was more to life, then you need this book. It will give you a new vision for your future, a vision that could change everything.

—PHIL COOKE
FILMMAKER, MEDIA CONSULTANT
AUTHOR OF *ONE BIG THING: DISCOVERING WHAT YOU WERE BORN TO DO*

In *No Regrets* Robin urgently reminds us of the brevity of our earthly days, the benefits of the inevitable times of suffering, and the ultimate blessing in choosing to live God's way. The book is chock-full of actionable keys and strategies that are sure to bring joy and fulfillment to every reader.

—DEBORAH SMITH PEGUES
BEST-SELLING AUTHOR OF
30 DAYS TO TAMING YOUR TONGUE
CEO/FOUNDER, THE PEGUES GROUP, INC.

Ordinary people go through extraordinary experiences. Through those times of trials and testing they learn an extraordinary message. Robin Bertram has been given that message. This book will encourage you to view life in such a way that every moment counts. Life is precious; embrace it.

—DEBORAH G. ROSS
DEBORAH ROSS MINISTRIES INC.
AUTHOR OF *HEALING A BROKEN MARRIAGE*,
WOMAN2WOMAN: THE NAOMI AND RUTH EXPERIENCE,
AND *SAVE IT! MARRIAGE BIBLE STUDY*

Robin Bertram, in *No Regrets*, shares her personal journey toward unwavering contentment, unshakable faith, and abundant joy. Every individual who wants to live life to the fullest, pleasing God and loving people, should read this book. It offers keys to living a rich life and reminds us to take time to embrace even the small day-to-day moments.

—Jack Watts
Award-Winning Author of *Hi, My Name Is Jack*

No Regrets is a page-turner and one of the most inspiring books I have come across in a long time. It encourages us to live in such a way that we will never have to regret decisions we make. Robin is a woman of prayer and deserves much credit for exploring topics in a novel way, one that not only instructs but also inspires. The concept of *No Regrets* is deep and inspiring, filled with wisdom-based insights that will warm your heart and encourage your faith.

—Sharon Hill
Author of *The OnCall Prayer Journal*
and *The Power of Three*

In a culture that seeks to convince us personal gain brings ultimate fulfillment, Robin Bertram proves the opposite. In *No Regrets* she uncovers the lies that would have us exchange the pursuit of the superficial for the greater reward of living passionately, loving unconditionally, and giving extravagantly.

Through candid stories, analogies, and personal transparency Robin Bertram reveals the truth about living with intention—that loving without limitations does not hinder us but liberates us to enjoy life the way it was designed to be, passionate and fulfilling.

—Tracey Mitchell
TV Host
Author of *Downside Up*

Thought-provoking and introspective, *No Regrets* will cause you to pause and cut out the noise of hectic living. Robin Bertram encourages intentional living with a forward-thinking mind-set rather than one that dwells on past regrets. With an emphasis on loving, living purposefully, and forgiving, this book is an excellent tool for everyone who wants to live a more fulfilling life.

—Wendie Pett
Fitness and Wellness Expert,
TV Host of *Visibly Fit TV*

I believe one of our failures as Christians living in today's culture has been our hesitation to write and leave our personal story for the next generation. Most of us have been silent, but Robin reminds us in *No Regrets* that our lives are short and our legacy matters. In this remarkable book she shares her story and encourages you to do the same. So what are you waiting for?

—KATHLEEN COOKE
WRITER, SPEAKER, AND COFOUNDER OF COOKE PICTURES
AND THE INFLUENCE LAB

Not everyone gets a second chance, but Robin, in *No Regrets*, does. She shares with transparency and sincerity her insight as she walked through this journey. This book will encourage you to evaluate your life and legacy and not wait until a tragedy occurs. Robin encourages the reader to accomplish their God-given assignments and move with power, passion, and prayer into a life with no regrets.

—JOAN HIGLEY
RIGHT WORD MINISTRY

One of the most significant takeaways of this book for me was the importance of building a spiritual legacy: build it, live it, and leave it. *No Regrets* encourages the reader to begin now by the way they walk, talk, and live and to become influential for Christ, and through their witness they can be impactful for the kingdom of God.

—SUELLEN ROBERTS
CHRISTIAN WOMEN IN MEDIA
FOUNDER AND PRESIDENT

Is it possible to live life with no regrets? Imagine living free from regret, having a life filled with boundless faith, and living a passionate, purposeful life. Learn how in Robin Bertram's powerful book, *No Regrets*.

—KATHLEEN HARDAWAY
AUTHOR OF *I KISSED A LOT OF FROGS*

NO
REGRETS

ROBIN M. BERTRAM

CHARISMA
HOUSE

Most CHARISMA HOUSE BOOK GROUP products are available at special quantity discounts for bulk purchase for sales promotions, premiums, fund-raising, and educational needs. For details, write Charisma House Book Group, 600 Rinehart Road, Lake Mary, Florida 32746, or telephone (407) 333-0600.

No REGRETS by Robin Bertram
Published by Charisma House
Charisma Media/Charisma House Book Group
600 Rinehart Road
Lake Mary, Florida 32746
www.charismahouse.com

Cover design by Studio Gearbox
Design Director: Justin Evans

Visit the author's website at RobinBertram.tv.

Library of Congress Cataloging-in-Publication Data:
An application to register this book for cataloging has been submitted to the Library of Congress.
International Standard Book Number: 978-1-62999-084-2
E-book ISBN: 978-1-62999-085-9

17 18 19 20 21 — 9 8 7 6 5 4 3 2 1
Printed in the United States of America

This book was a gift from God: He gave it, and I now give back to Him. I dedicate it to God first. It is only by His mercy that I am alive today.

I also dedicate it to my father, Paul A. Maddy, who inspired me, through a life well lived, to write it. It was his godly legacy and the impact he had on my life that allowed me to become who I am today. I also dedicate this work to Ruth H. Maddy, my mother, who stood by my father's side for nearly sixty years. She taught me about the importance of having a generous, loving heart. I also dedicate this book to my dear, sweet family: Ken, Logan, Kelsey, Taylor, and Ben, who stood by me during the darkest, most difficult days of my life. It was through their love and support that I pressed forward.

No Regrets is a celebration of life, an invitation to love deeply and live passionately, and an encouragement to live the kind of life that will impact generations.

To God be all the glory, all the honor, and all the praise.

CONTENTS

ACKNOWLEDGMENTS

I WOULD LIKE TO acknowledge my husband, Ken, who helped me throughout this process; my children, Logan and Taylor, who have been my driving force; my father, who gave me a love for the Word; and all the friends and family who stood beside me during this season of my life. I am eternally grateful.

FOREWORD

THE WORDS FOUND in this book echo sweet sounds in my heart. As soon as I heard them, I was reminded of the words of this old song, "Life is like a mountain railroad with an engineer that's brave. We must make the run successful from the cradle to the grave."[1] There are so many ups and downs, swerves and curves, mountains and valleys in our lives that all of us experience. Sometimes we don't know up from down and where to turn around. But I'm so excited to step into the pages of this book and take a journey through the tunnels and hills and mountains and valleys of life with a lady I have known for nearly a decade through praying together, presenting through the Christian Women in Media Association, and watching each other's journeys through some of these mountains and valleys, learning how to walk through the valley of the shadow of death and have no regrets. Remember, we are traveling *through* the tunnels; we're not parking.

As Robin writes from her heart to us, she is demonstrating the value of strengthening and encouraging others to live a life of significance in spite of the terrain.

Regrets are inevitable in this uncertain world. I've often said, "I wish someone would have told me..." Or perhaps, "I wish I had listened to that someone!" Maybe my expectations in marriage would have been more accurate. Or I would have planned my finances differently. My diet would have fueled my health sufficiently. And the thoughts go on and on. Robin writes out of personal experiences that prove to us the benefits of growing through these twists and turns and looking in our souls for the maps to put us on a journey of no regrets.

At seventy-five years of age I frequently review my life of not having a legal birth name until I was in my late thirties, but I still look back through the decades and say to God, "Thank You, Father, because though I was un-named for those years, You knew my name. No regrets. Even though I've lived with a blood disorder and cancer and a stroke, You walked me through the months of failing health. You walked me through when the doctors had given up on me and I could only turn to You. No regrets!"

Oh sure, I've lived a part of my life with lack of forgiveness, with my feelings hurt, with business struggles, with family issues, with ministry issues, and with a blurred mind without an understanding. But when I allowed God to take complete control of my ups and downs and ins and outs, He showed me how to live with no regrets!

Read this purposeful and powerful direction for a safe journey through the tunnels of life led by the engineer of life who makes the run successful from the cradle to the grave, and live with no regrets.

—Rev. Dr. Thelma Wells (Mama T)
President of A Woman of God Ministries and
Generation Love: Divine Explosion
Author, Speaker, Professor

PREFACE

ON HIS DEATHBED my father said, "Robin, I have no regrets." It took me years to understand what he meant by that statement. It became much clearer to me when I faced my own mortality. We all acknowledge that we will die one day, but it's different when you actually face that day, particularly when it's much sooner than you had ever imagined. You will have a new perspective, and that perspective will change the way you live your life. I had that epiphany.

I wrote *No Regrets* to share the powerful life lessons and wisdom learned through my journey and to express the importance of living today with great joy while making every moment really count. It is my hope that this book will inspire, motivate, and encourage you to begin to walk a life of love, peace, joy, and faith with gratitude. It will encourage you to develop an intimate prayer life, to develop a willingness to forgive, to embrace every good gift you've been given with a thankful heart, and to live life to the fullest because no one is guaranteed tomorrow.

I hope to encourage you to move out of your own comfort zone and truly live for Christ, and by doing so, you will be finding greater fulfillment as you begin to view your life from a heavenly perspective. How? Through the truth found in Scripture combined with the insight gained from real-life stories with victorious outcomes. *No Regrets* will encourage you to forgive, to love deeply, to mend broken relationships, and to build a legacy now so that when the day comes, there will be a strong spiritual legacy to leave behind.

INTRODUCTION

SAMANTHA PEERED INTO the mirror one day and saw a woman looking back at her whom she did not even recognize. "Can this really be my life?" she asked herself. "This is not the way I thought things were going to turn out." Her adult children had little interest in her life, her husband was not meeting her personal needs, and her career had not materialized into the success she so desperately wanted. "If only" kept running through her mind. "If only I had attended a better college. If only I had married a different man. If only I had spent more time with my children..."

While your life may not be like Samantha's, without a doubt every one of us can think of times in life when we've experienced regret and wished we could just do it all over again. Though the past cannot be changed, I'm telling you with great certainty that your future can. It can take a different course if you live intentionally. Living intentionally means having a plan, a course of action, that will help to chart out your days in such a way that you will learn to embrace and enjoy all the good that life has to offer. And then you can decide to make it happen. It can be a future that is absent of regret and lived to the fullest, embracing the small things of life with great joy, contentment, and satisfaction, all the while honoring God and honoring people. You can live the life you were created to live.

This book addresses this very issue of backward thinking instead of forward living. We all can get so caught up in what we did or didn't do that we forget to embrace and enjoy today. Not only that, but our regretful thinking can steal our tomorrows as well. Today is the best day you have; it is not yesterday because you cannot change it, and not tomorrow because it may never come. No matter what stage of life you are in, how young or old you are, what you have or have not accomplished thus far, you can begin today to live your life intentionally for Christ, and doing so will minimize regrets and maximize personal fulfillment. Release your yesterday, embrace your today, and confidently and intentionally decide to live your tomorrow with purpose and direction as you begin to build a legacy worth leaving behind.

Throughout this book you will find keys that will prepare you to make the best life choices, to live biblically, and to leave a legacy that will far outlast the number of your days. The circumstances and situations that cause regret or solidify our destiny begin with the decisions and choices we make today.

Within this book you will find:

+ Pillars of Abundant Living: These contain specific scriptures which have given me comfort, wisdom, and insight during my personal journey.

+ Intentional Living: At the end of each chapter there are several keys that will help you become more intentional in living your life for Christ and embracing today.

+ Shareworthy: There are text boxes scattered throughout each chapter that include quotes expanding on the ideas in this book that are worth sharing on your social media platforms.

+ The Thirty-Day Love Challenge: At the end of the book (appendix) there is a love challenge, which will help you personally evaluate your own love walk on a daily basis for thirty days so that you can honestly get a picture of where you are and where you can grow.

May God fill your heart with abundant joy as you come along with me on this journey. May your days be bright and fulfilling as you choose to serve and honor God with your time, talent, and resources. May your years be long and fruitful for His kingdom, His honor, and His glory, and may you accomplish all that He has sent you here to do.

PART I

BUILD A LEGACY

Chapter 1

LIVE LIKE YOU WERE DYING

Merely to live among men requires of us years of hard toil and much care and attention to the things of this world. In sharp contrast to this is our life in the Spirit. There we enjoy another and higher kind of life; we are children of God; we possess heavenly status and enjoy intimate fellowship with Christ.

—A. W. Tozer[1]

On his deathbed my father looked me in the eye and said, "Robin, I have no regrets." That statement puzzled me. I was confused at the time. As I began to think about his statement, I quickly recognized that I already had plenty of regrets in my own life. I wondered, "How do you live your life in such a way that you can truly say, 'I have no regrets'?" I pondered that statement for some time. I knew my father. He was a quiet, loving man, but he was not perfect. He had successes and failures, just like everyone else. He was a very hard worker. He loved God, and he loved life. He loved the small things in life. He loved Maddy's mountain, our homeplace in Virginia, and he loved the outdoors. He loved a good meal; I guess that's where I developed a love for preparing great dinners for my family. He instilled in me a love for God and a love for family. He loved to play the piano and sing, and he loved people. But how could he say that he had no regrets?

At some point we will all die. That inevitable reality should be a wake-up call. Will we be able to say that we paid attention to the most important things in life, or will we look back with deep regret and wish we could just have a do-over? Will we be able to say that we lived life to its fullest, or will we say that we did just enough to get by?

Truth be told, most of us live as though we will always have tomorrow, but we absolutely do not have that assurance. We don't know how or when death may come. We can't simply put off being the person God wants us to be and avoid doing what He has called us to do. We can't rely on tomorrows or somedays. My friend, someday may not come. I want to encourage you: take this day and make it the best day ever. Live it as if you will not have tomorrow.

"Lord, make me to know my end, and what is the measure of my days, that I may know how transient I am" (Ps. 39:4). This verse and its prayer were going to be brought to fruition in my life. Along with it I was going to get an answer to the question I had regarding my father's deathbed statement, but not in the way I had expected. I had been a healthy person all my life; I never had much more than a cold or occasional flu. My diet was fairly good because I preferred cooking at home instead of eating out; therefore I was cognizant about the quality of the meals I would prepare. I was healthy. I did not drink alcohol. I was not a smoker. I did not even drink soft drinks, but rather tea, coffee, and mostly water. My biggest addiction was popcorn at the movies. I know, it's terrible. I loved going to movies, and I loved eating popcorn. Outside of that, I did most of the right things to maintain a healthy lifestyle. Nevertheless, one day my life changed in a very significant way.

TUSCANY

Several years ago I was preparing to go on a family vacation to Italy. We were going to stay in Florence and the Tuscan countryside. My family had traveled to Rome several years earlier, and it had been one of our favorite vacations. I woke up in the middle of the night several weeks before we were to leave and my right arm felt strange. It felt very weak, and it was a chore just to lift it up. Days before I had volunteered to help a friend paint her bedroom, so I just assumed it was a pinched nerve. I dismissed it as a non-issue. But as the days went on, there was no improvement.

My extended family came in for my daughter's graduation party from NC State, which was just two days before we were to leave for Italy. I tried to pick up a drinking glass, and it felt as if I were lifting a ton of bricks. I could hardly pick up the glass. The house was overflowing with out-of-town guests, and my home was filled with joy and laughter. However, my niece was very concerned about my arm and convinced me to go to the urgent care facility. The entire time I was thinking, "This is such a waste of time." I had so much to do in preparation for our trip.

The nurse took me back, asked a few questions, and then promptly left the room. The urgent care doctor came in almost immediately. He asked a few more questions and then with a very grim look on his face he said, "I'm sorry, but this is neurological." It didn't even register to me what that meant. I thought to myself, "No, I'm a healthy person. I am not sick. I just have a little issue with my arm." He gave me a few potential diagnoses of what it could be: a stroke, an aneurysm, MS, or the deadly, incurable, intensely painful ALS. WHAT? It pains me even to write those words.

Then he continued, "But I feel certain it was not a stroke." He told me to get in to see a doctor as soon as I returned from my trip and indicated that it would be a process of elimination to get a diagnosis. They would rule out one thing at a time.

"So teach us to number our days, that we may apply our hearts to wisdom" (Ps. 90:12). The Lord was certainly doing this in my life.

I gathered my things and left the doctor's office in complete shock. Thoughts flew through my head. "This cannot be happening to me. This is really serious. I do not believe this. He must be wrong. I'm too young to be having a serious and potentially deadly disease. I have too much to do. I haven't reached my goals in life." The shock I felt was overwhelming. The packing was finished, the guests were on their way out, and I sat in my home as if I were in some weird comatose state of being. I couldn't even think. I was so overwhelmed at even the possibility of having a serious disease that I could not move. After what seemed like hours my husband said to me, "Everything is going to be fine. We are going on this trip, and we will get you to a doctor when we get home." Vacation? Are you kidding me? But he convinced me it would be the best for all, so I acquiesced.

We flew into Florence and drove the hour and a half into the countryside. The home we had rented was lovely. It was on a mountain overlooking all of Tuscany. The fireplace was in the dining room and a large, wide-planked rustic table sat in front of it. The home was located in a working olive grove, complete with ducks, chickens, pigs, and of course, plenty of phenomenal olive oil. Oh, I can't forget the boar prosciutto or snails, both considered true delicacies in Tuscany. The home had all the charm you might expect from such a beautiful, lush region. Its owner was just as charming. Francesco was a true Tuscan in every sense of the word. He was an artist who had quite a flare for the dramatic. Books about his work were prominently displayed on the sideboard in the dining room for all the guests to see.

Bronze statues dotted the entire property, including a huge urn that represented a mother's womb. I gazed down at the statue with a perplexed look on my face. With broken English Francesco explained that it contained his mother-in-law's ashes. Strange, I know, but quite interesting. When he explained what it was, he had to wipe the tears from his eyes, even though she had been gone for a number of years.

Everyone was so excited to be there. Each day we would take long trips to different towns, mostly fortresses from years gone by dotted on what seemed to be every hillside. At night we would come back to our home. We would light a fire in the fireplace and play games or have a late dinner.

Lights Out

But at night, when the lights went out, my face would hit my pillow and I would cry out to God almost the entire night. My pillow would be drenched in tears. "God, why? Why, God? Why?" The pain was unbearable. I begged God to please let me live. I begged God to take this away. I begged God to please heal my body, all the while feeling totally abandoned by Him. I felt completely empty. I felt alone. I felt as if my Creator did not care about me. But deep inside I knew He was truly there to hear my cries.

The first thoughts that ran through my head were of my children. "What will my children do? They need their mother in their lives. Who will love them? Who will pray for them? Who will be there to support them throughout their lives? Who will be with my daughter when she gives birth to her first child? What if I can't attend her wedding? And my son, who is going to help him? Who will pray for him, love him, and encourage him?"

Grandchildren. I kept thinking, "I want grandchildren. I want the privilege of seeing my children with children of their own." I thought of my nieces and nephews, whom I love dearly. "What if I can't be there to encourage them? Who's going to love them unconditionally?"

Holidays were next to run through my mind: "Who will have Christmas? Who will put up the Christmas tree?"

My best friend: "What if we can't travel together anymore? We have had such a tremendous time traveling around the world. Everywhere we go someone asks, 'Are you two sisters?' which is a very funny question because we look nothing at all alike. We have a special chemistry, and people can sense the joy when we are out on one of our excursions. Who will take my place? My BFF and I have been doing life together. Who's going to be there for my best friend?"

These were the agonizing, gut-wrenching, extremely painful questions that kept running through my mind. And then I would have a random thought such as, "There are certain foods I've not eaten enough of yet. What if I can't eat fettuccini carbonara again, ever? Or a really good steak? Or cheese grits? (I love cheese grits; it's a Southern thing.) I know that there is food in heaven (Matt. 8:11), but is it the same?" I know that sounds strange, but these thoughts literally flooded my mind. "What if I can no longer walk, or lift my arms, or dress myself? What if I cannot get to the beach again? Who will love my little Sophie? (Who, by the way, is the sweetest little Yorkie you've ever seen, and needs lots of love.)

"Who will…?" I kept asking. I was exhausted. I couldn't sleep at night and couldn't stop during the day. I felt angry. Angry I was sick. Angry that God had let this happen to me. Angry that I had tried to serve Him and He still let this happen. I was just plain angry. I didn't want to miss out on our time together as a family and the memories that were being created either. It was a tough call, but ultimately I was very glad I pushed through.

I had to face my own mortality. Truly, before this incident, I felt as if I would just go on forever. Little did I know, when I got to a doctor, I would be given a potential death sentence with no chance of recovery and told I may die within two years. There was no cure, and there was no treatment. For one entire year of my life I waited to die.

Shareworthy

We are all faced with a series of great opportunities brilliantly disguised as impossible situations.

—Chuck Swindoll[2]

WAKE-UP CALL

Can you imagine? Perhaps not, but it was a real wake-up call for me. I thought of all those things I wanted to do but never got around to doing. I thought about the places I wanted to go, the people I wanted to see, the work I wanted to accomplish. Now everything was on hold.

My friend Claire was a brilliant woman in her mid-sixties who had worked as an accountant for a large real estate agent in Raleigh, North Carolina. She lived a rather meager life due to choices she had made early on. She had been in relatively good health but began having some issues with her shoulder. She gave me a call one day and asked if she could come over for prayer. As we were praying, I sensed in my heart that I was to tell her to "get your house in order." After we finished praying, I shared with her the impression the Lord had given me. We finished praying and she went home. Several days later she went to her doctor to have him check her shoulder and complained that she had been feeling tired. The results of the tests he ordered were clear: she had stage-IV lung cancer. Three months later Claire was dead.

Wake-up call.

We see things like this happen to others, but we never think it will happen to us. We have all had loved ones, friends, or neighbors whose lives have been cut short, but we never really gave it much thought. My friend, now is the time to give it thought. What if your days on this earth were cut short? Would your house be in order? Would you be able to say that you lived a life that pleased God? Have you placed the right priority on the most important things? Could you say at the end of your days that you lived your life in such a way that you have no regrets? If not, then you can change that reality. You can take each day and live it as if it were your last.

Shareworthy

Let those who thoughtfully consider the brevity of life remember the length of eternity.

—Thomas Ken[3]

LIFE IS BUT A VAPOR

"You do not know what will happen tomorrow. What is your life? It is just a vapor that appears for a little while and then vanishes away" (James 4:14). Your life is but a vapor. It appears for a little time and then it vanishes. If you have seventy or eighty years, you are blessed. You are given one shot and only one. You have to make the very best of the life you've been given. You cannot determine the length of your days; that's already been determined (Ps. 139:16). There is a time to live and a time to die (Eccles. 3:2). You can, however, determine the kind of life you want to live. No matter how long you live, life is short. You can't truly understand the importance of what I am saying until you face your own mortality or perhaps lose someone very close to you unexpectedly. But you can find great joy in knowing that regardless of your length of days, you can live your life to the fullest, embracing the very best it has to offer, by becoming the person God wants you to be and accomplishing all God has for you to do.

What would you change if you had only a short while to live? How different would your day look? Would you take more time to spend with family and friends? Would you pay more attention to the small things in life? Would you find moments of joy that you otherwise would have missed?

Recently someone very dear to me said, "I don't want my next forty years to be like my last forty years." I asked, "Then what do you intend to change?" If we want a different outcome, we have to do things differently.

Childhood Memories

When I was a little girl, I remember going to Monterey, Virginia, for the Maple Syrup Festival each year. The festival was considered to be "Virginia's Sweet Spot." It was like taking a step back in time. Buckets dotted the mountainside; they were strategically placed under taps that were drilled into the maple trees where they were still "opened" by hand. After the sugar water is gathered, it is cooked over a fire in an open pan and then transferred into an iron kettle to finish.

We went every year, and the day was always filled with fond memories. It was such a big deal to me. We would get up early in the morning and make the drive in the spring of the year. I loved to look at the beautiful flowers that were just starting to bloom. I loved the buckwheat pancakes that were offered up. They even had a Maple Syrup Queen. Yes, you heard me; a beauty pageant was held in honor of the festival and a winner was crowned. I loved the smell of maple syrup in the air and the candy (lots of candy). Maple doughnuts, maple pit-cooked BBQ, pork skins, and those delicious pancakes were the highlight of the festival in my mind. Sweet memories. When was the last time you shared memorable moments like these with those you love?

Why Wait?

As adults we often forget the fun things. We forget the events that brought us joy as a child, and we become so busy in life we forget to enjoy it and to help our families enjoy it. Often it takes a major life crisis to get us to the point of understanding that life is short and we have to embrace every moment with joy.

Why wait? Why not embrace all that life has to offer and live your life in such a way that you too can say, "I have no regrets"? Why not decide today that you won't need a crisis to enjoy life to its fullest, but instead that you are going to love living? Love it, no matter the circumstances.

Pillar of Abundant Living

I perceived that there is nothing better for them than to be joyful and to do good as long as they live; also that everyone should eat and drink and take pleasure in all his toil—this is God's gift to man.

—Ecclesiastes 3:12–13, ESV

Most of us know what we need to change, what we want to change, and what we can change so that we can live the life God wants us to live. Perhaps for you it's not about changing anything. I know that when my death sentence was handed down, I realized I wanted to get more out of life and to put more into life. I began to press into God more. I began to love more. I began to laugh more. I began to notice the small things in life more. I began to celebrate more. I began to treasure my days more, and instead of just getting through my daily schedule with all the time constraints and deadlines, I began to embrace life.

A New Lease on Life

When the year of waiting to die was up, I went back to the Mayo Clinic. Tests were run. Inexplicably there was no sign of the disease and no further damage. A year and a half later the Mayo Clinic released me with no explanation because they could not determine what had happened to me. To say I was relieved would be a huge understatement. However, during that first year I had to deal with many internal struggles regarding end-of-life issues. One question that continually came to mind was, "What makes life worth living for me?"

Slowly the answers came. I realized that living a life that has worth and value is living a life that pleases God. I learned the importance of loving deeply. I learned how to forgive without reservation. I learned to treasure the little things in life. I learned who I was and what I truly believed. I learned to have a heart of gratitude, and most importantly I learned how to surrender.

Not only did the issue with my health change the way I think about day-to-day living, but it also gave me a new perspective on life. It gave me a desire to accomplish the God-inspired goals I had conveniently put on hold. It gave me the impetus to finish projects that had been on my heart for years. It gave me a desire to say "thank you" more often and mean it. I wanted to dance more, sing more, laugh more, and love more. I ask you, "Why wait?" Why not live this day as though it were your last? In this book I hope to impart to you just how you can do that—whether you have one day left on this earth or many years ahead of you.

As Warren Wiersbe said, "You do not move ahead by constantly looking in a rearview mirror. The past is a rudder to guide you, not an anchor to drag you. We must learn from the past but not live in the past." [4]

Intentional Living

- Make a list of childhood memories that you really enjoyed.
- Make a video with an iPad or iPhone and tell about each one of those stories.
- Put the videos on a flash drive and give them to your family members as a keepsake.
- If you have children, plan at least once a week to do something with them that you enjoyed doing when you were a child.
- Make plans for several generations of your family to celebrate a family day.
- Decide in your heart to enjoy every day; your days are numbered.
- Laugh like a child again; it makes the heart merry and is good for your soul.

CHAPTER 2

TESTS AND MEASUREMENTS

If man had his way, the plan of redemption would be an endless and bloody conflict. In reality, salvation was bought not by Jesus' fist, but by His nail-pierced hands; not by muscle but by love; not by vengeance but by forgiveness; not by force but by sacrifice. Jesus Christ our Lord surrendered in order that He might win; He destroyed His enemies by dying for them and conquered death by allowing death to conquer Him.

—A. W. TOZER[1]

WHEN I WAS in my senior year at college, I took a postgraduate class in psychology called Tests and Measurements. It was a class designed to adequately prepare the student with a solid understanding of various kinds of psychological tests; the ability to develop, administer, and interpret tests; and the knowledge of measurement theory, which included reliability and validity. I found the class to be very interesting. We were learning how to analyze cognitive functioning, compare and contrast constructs of intelligence and achievement, and analyze measures of emotional and behavioral function. There were many factors that were taken into consideration regarding the reliability and validity of the tests given.

Probability and Statistics was truly my least favorite class. I found it rather difficult to understand; however, when it came to applying statistics to psychological test data, I got it. I know that may sound odd, but when it came to practical application, it all seemed to make sense to me. Any test is only as good as the ability to adequately calculate its reliability and validity. The best outcome is achieved when you compare a fluid measurement to a benchmark or point of reference that has been set and is unchangeable. The benchmark is the standard by which all other measurements are assessed.

The study of human behavior and the mind was fascinating to me. It was so intriguing to look at why people behave as they do. Recently I was talking with a man who said to me, "I know for certain I would be willing to die for Christ." I paused for just a moment and then asked, "But will you be willing to live for Him?" He took a deep breath and said, "That's a very good question." What makes a person decide that they would be willing to die for someone or something but would not be fully devoted to live for that same someone or something? Ironic, isn't it?

MEASURES OF COMPARISON

In my studies the term *metrics* was a quantitative term regarding parameters or measures of assessment used for comparison or to track performance in a given situation. What do you use as your metrics, your personal measurement or benchmark, when it comes to setting your own standards in life? Most people compare their standards to those of family members, others in their lives, or even to societal mores.

We often believe that we are living better than so-and-so; therefore we must be OK. I talked with a father who was convinced most of his life that he was doing better as a father than his father did. His measure: "My dad never went to one of my baseball games. I go to all of my son's games." Yet there was an obvious void in their relationship, and he failed to acknowledge his own personal shortcomings because relatively speaking, in his mind, he was doing better than his own dad and he thought he had turned out OK. This form of relativism is clearly in error.

What measure are you using? Are you determined to think that all is well because you are not doing what your dad or mom did? Perhaps you are a pretty upstanding person in the community: well known, well liked, and successful. Do you determine your values by what society says is acceptable? People change. Leaders change. Societies change. God's Word never changes.

Paradise Lost

In British literature there is an epic poem titled *Paradise Lost*, written in the seventeenth century by John Milton. He was dubbed the greatest poet of his time. It is a story of the battle between good and evil, light and dark, God and Satan. It was based on the biblical account of the fall of man, the temptation of Adam and Eve by the fallen angel Satan, and the expulsion from the Garden of Eden. Milton stated his purpose for writing the epic poem was to justify the ways of God to man.[2]

The story opens with Satan and his followers in hell after being defeated in a battle with God and ends with Adam and Eve being expelled from the garden, but only after receiving the revelation that God would send a Savior into the world to pay for the sins of man.

I took a literature class, and my assignment was to do a literary critical analysis of *Paradise Lost*. After working tirelessly on the assignment, I was shocked and surprised when I got the paper back and had been given a C. What? I loved working on that assignment and had spent well beyond my normal effort in writing it, but nonetheless my professor obviously was unimpressed. Under the letter grade he had written a note. It said, "Stop by my office. I want to discuss your work." Later that week I dropped by for our meeting. As I entered his office and sat down in a chair adjacent to his desk, he smiled and said, "Robin, no one can see things [life] in such black and white. I want you to go back and rewrite your paper." So I did. I turned my paper back in the following week. He re-graded it and this time gave me a B. I had been graded on the conceptual aspect of the paper, and unfortunately for me he could not see things as clearly as I did. My grammar was pretty clean, but my concept, in his mind, was not. In my mind there is no gray, only black and white. It's easier to live that way. No confusion, just clarity.

Milton was devout in his beliefs, although at times unorthodox. The heart of the work was right on. His desire was to vindicate God's actions to man, to emphasize the results of disobedience, and to declare the eternal providence of God. It isn't that God's actions need justification but that man needs help understanding the justice in His actions. Milton attempted to portray to man that the fall, death, and salvation are all acts of a just God.

Today we still have this same argument. If God is a loving God, how can He...? Fill in the blank. But He is just, and He gives us His plumb line, His standard of measurement, which is His written Word. It is not what your neighbors are doing or not doing. It is not what society says is acceptable. It is not what our government sanctions. Instead it is His Word, written by holy men under the inspiration of the Holy Spirit. It is infallible, and it is His Word that is the benchmark. His Word is never changing. It will always be the same, and you can trust in its reliability and consistency for all of eternity.

As I asked the man who said he would die for Christ but paused in answering the question, "Will you live for Christ?," I ask you. Will you live for Christ? Have you dedicated your life to Christ? Have you given Him leadership in your life? Are you just calling yourself "Christian," or are you a true disciple and follower of Christ? If not, today is the day of salvation (2 Cor. 6:2). Today is the day you can wipe away all those regrets you've been carrying around for far too long. Today is the day that you can put your past in the past, and let God direct your future.

What is your benchmark? The Word of God tells us we all fall short of the glory of God (Rom. 3:23). Here the playing field is level. We all fall short; that's you and that's me. There is none who is righteous according to God's standard. We all are like filthy rags in His sight, not one clean enough, good enough, or righteous enough to stand before a holy God (Isa. 64:6). How do you measure up?

If you are like me, I didn't measure up at all. I fell short. I could see that my way of living was displeasing to God, and therefore I needed a Savior. I needed a Savior because I just could not be good enough. Neither can you. If we hold ourselves up in comparison to our friends or neighbors, then possibly we think we are good enough, or maybe not. It would depend on who is doing the judging and how accurately the judge could analyze our actions. The good news is if we accept Jesus as Lord and believe in our hearts and confess with our mouths that He is Lord, then we will be saved (Rom. 10:9).

God judges us not by our standards but by His. All sin has a price, and that price is death. His righteous Son, Jesus Christ of Nazareth, paid the price for our sins. As we confess our sins, repent, turn from them, and submit to God in obedience to His Word, we are assured of eternal life through Jesus Christ. The *old you* is replaced by the *new you*, and your righteousness is now determined by blood sacrificed by a sinless Savior, not by all the sins that you have committed in your lifetime. I don't know about you, but I choose to be judged by the righteousness of Christ instead of my own righteousness, or the lack thereof.

Shareworthy

Narrow all your interests until your mind, heart, and body are focused on Jesus Christ.
—Oswald Chambers[3]

God sets the standard. We have to go by His measure, not the metrics we set for ourselves. In *Paradise Lost* Milton focused on the first sin of man: his disobedience to the directives of God. He argued that there is a hierarchy in which the inferior are to obey the superior. When Adam and Eve sinned, they defied the natural order of things and caused great chaos. Every time we sin, it causes chaos in our lives. Maybe not at that very moment, but eventually it always catches up.

SWEET CAROLINE

Caroline was a sweet Southern woman. She was the type of lady who always had something to offer you to eat when you stopped by her home. Whether it was fresh, hot biscuits served up with homemade jam, a piece of apple pie, or cold iced tea with lemon, she knew how to make her guests feel right at home. She was a churchgoing woman and attended a small Seventh-Day Adventist church in the little town in Virginia where she lived. Caroline was a frail woman of very small stature. She struggled with breathing difficulties most of her life. As she aged, her health issues continued to escalate. Even though she didn't attend my father's church, one day my father got a call. Caroline had been hospitalized and was not expected to make it. My dad called and asked me to go to the hospital with him to visit Caroline. When we got there, the doctor explained that she had flatlined and it took several attempts to bring her back. We visited Caroline for the next several days. In a conversation with my dad and me, she explained that when she flatlined, she was certain that she was not going to heaven. She said, "It was very gray and then dark. I am certain I was not going to make it to heaven. I know that I was on my way to hell."

Pillar of Abundant Living

For I say to you that unless your righteousness exceeds the righteousness of the scribes and Pharisees, you will in no way enter the kingdom of heaven.

—Matthew 5:20

I thought to myself, "This precious woman had probably lived as good a life as anyone I've ever known. She was kind. She was loving. She was generous. Yet she was on her way to hell. Wow. Not by my judgment but by her own testimony." My father and I stood by her bedside and shared the plan of salvation with her. He asked her, "Caroline, are you willing to allow Jesus to be the Lord of your life?"

"Oh, yes," she said. "Oh, yes!" Caroline passed away several weeks after that, which was very sad, but fortunately we had witnessed her deathbed conversion. Caroline made the right decision. Many do not have such an opportunity. Deathbed conversions are a tremendous act of God's mercy. There are those who will neglect the Lord's invitation until the Lord says, "I will not strive forever with man." There comes a time in your life when you must decide if you will serve God or serve Satan. These are the only two choices, and your decision will matter for eternity. Whom will you serve?

Radical Life Change

We have to think about all those people we know who are refusing to serve God and how utterly empty their lives really are. They may look on the outside as though they have it all together, but on the inside they are dead. I had the opportunity to pray with a young, handsome man in his late twenties. His name was Ian. He came to my church for prayer ministry. My prayer partner and I began to pray for this man, and immediately I sensed in my spirit that he had made a covenant with the devil. Trust me, that is not the norm for prayer ministry. However, I proceeded with that line of questioning. Ian was about to experience a God-encounter. I asked him why he had decided to serve Satan. The young man looked at me with astonishment and said, "How did you know that?" I told him that the Lord had shown me in my spirit. He began to weep. He had been searching for a church in the middle of the week when he ran into a police officer who recommended that he come to our church. He told me that he was on the way to commit suicide. The word that I had been given in prayer was the impetus God used to encourage him to open his heart to the Lord for salvation. He repented of his sins, renounced his covenant with Satan, and asked the Lord to forgive him and become the Lord of his life. His heart was radically changed that day, and he went on to be a missionary in Mexico. So I ask this day, whom will you serve?

This life is a journey, and it is one that can be snatched right out of our hands. When my life looked as if it would be cut short, I remember thinking, "There are so many things I want to do for the Lord, and I haven't completed my work." I want to ask you: If your life were being cut short, what would you think about? What would you want to get done? Trust me, your vision will change when faced with the possibility of not being here. You will want to finish things. You will want to take care of those things that have been put on hold because of time constraints or just because there has been a lack of correct priorities. What is your priority? If you are not saved, then your priority should be salvation. If you are saved, then it should be helping others become saved by sharing with them your personal story and the message of the gospel: the death, burial, and resurrection of Jesus Christ.

ABIDING

Once you are born again, to live a life of value, meaning, and purpose, you need to abide in His presence. Jesus said, "If you abide in Me, and My words abide in you, ask whatever you wish, and it will be done for you" (John 15:7, NASB).

There is a life-altering effect of being in His presence, and salvation is the first step in having a God-encounter. You may have had a visitation, but before salvation there was no communication. There are powerful benefits of being in His presence, which is practiced with day-by-day commitment to the cause of Christ. Do you need your prayers to be answered? I sure do, and I am thankful that we have His promise of answered prayers as we abide in Him. Abiding does not mean sitting idly by. It means resting in the work, resting in the moment, resting in the truth, resting in the confidence that God is your provision. He is your sustenance. He is your healer. He is your deliverer. He is your stronghold. He is your protector in the midst of every trouble or hardship in which you may find yourself. The abiding place is a place of peace and joy, and it is a place in which you determine to live your life in such a way that you no longer strive but instead rest with continual assurance of His goodness.

Helen Keller once said, "Deep, solemn optimism, it seems to me, should spring from this firm belief in the presence of God in the individual; not a remote, unapproachable governor of the universe, but a God who is very near every one of us, who is present not only in earth, sea and sky, but also in every pure and noble impulse of our hearts."[5]

There is a radical and transforming effect of being in His presence. Salvation is the beginning, and from that point on God-encounters are to occur and continue throughout the life of a believer, constantly bringing each of us into a higher level of spiritual consciousness, constantly sharpening our spiritual senses, constantly challenging our complacency and status quo mentality. It is to look at the Word of God and find meaning and application to your personal journey, and then live it out. Everything written in the Bible is your road map. There is only one way to find your particular path, and that is to earnestly dedicate time, energy, and prayer to the process, and through that commitment you will reach your intended destiny and experience a life of meaning and purpose along the way.

Practicing being in the presence of God will help you break with the past and establish a new direction and commitment wherever you may be in your journey. As you do, you will begin to find the true zeal and passion in spending time with God, and you will also grow in your desire to be in His presence and in His Word.

ONE GOD ENCOUNTER

There is no clearer picture of being in the presence of God, and the radical change that comes along with such a visitation, than the account we find in Acts 9:1–22. Let's explore the radical transformation of the life of Paul through a God-encounter, as he saw the glory of the Lord. Here we see a man who was going about his business, on his own path, determining his own allegiance, until he had a radical God-encounter. He was very comfortable. He was an educated man who sat under the great teacher of the law, Gamaliel (Acts 22:3). Therefore he had developed a tremendous respect for what was written. He was highly regarded within the confines of the Jewish religious system. His father was a Pharisee, meaning his father was scholarly and well versed in Scripture, as was he (Acts 23:6). His father and mother were both native Jews. He was a "Hebrew of Hebrews," as he referred to himself (Phil. 3:5). Paul, through his dramatic conversion on the road to Damascus, became determined to live his life for the cause of Christ, no matter the cost.

There are some things that broke off Paul because of this single God-encounter. A new path was determined by this encounter. A new passion was stirred through this encounter. A new name was given through this encounter. A divine mission was given through this encounter. A clean break with ritual and religiosity happened through this encounter.

The apostle Paul was on the road to Damascus that day to find Christians, those of the Way, to bring them back to Jerusalem and throw them in prison or even have them killed for their belief in Jesus Christ. Paul's objective was to stop the Christian effort. He had sent letters to the synagogues in Damascus to seek out those who believed, but on the way he had a God-encounter and came into the presence of a holy God. (See Acts 9:1–22.)

Have you had a real God-encounter? Are you born again? This is the most important decision you will ever make, and making it can lead to a life of no regrets. God will always reveal Himself in a true God-encounter through the power of the Holy Spirit and Jesus Christ, His Son.

As with the apostle Paul, one God-encounter can radically change the direction of your life forever. In a true God-encounter God's presence is tangible. It is weighty. When Paul, who was called Saul before his conversion, fell to the ground and heard, "Saul, Saul, why do you persecute Me?" and then after asking about the voice, heard, "I am Jesus, whom you are persecuting," those with Paul could also hear the voice of Jesus, and they stood speechless (Acts 9:4–7). They were in awe, afraid to move, afraid to speak, and afraid to be disruptive in any way. There was an overwhelming sense of His power and presence to which everyone paid attention.

In God's presence there is an emptying that occurs. We are emptied of our pride. We are emptied of our selfishness, self-indulgence, and hard-heartedness. We are emptied of our religiosity. We see ourselves for who we really are. We put all of our life's regrets, our sins, and our failures at the foot of the cross and literally have a new beginning.

Through his encounter with God the mind-sets that had blinded Paul were washed away. He was cleansed from a murderous spirit. He was emptied of all the hatred and condemnation against the Way. He was freed from religious chains of legalism and religiosity. Paul's eyes were opened. The scales fell off. The binding, blinding system of dead religion had lost its power, and he was a new creature in Christ. The old things had passed away. A true encounter with the living God will break the spirit of religiosity, empty man of his pride, and conform even the most vile and wicked into a living vessel for His glory.

Pillar of Abundant Living

For I am not ashamed of the gospel of Christ. For it is the power of God for salvation to everyone who believes, to the Jew first, and also to the Greek.

—Romans 1:16

LIFE IN BLACK AND WHITE

My takeaway from *Paradise Lost* was that life can be black and white, with absolutes that are written on our hearts. I have not changed my position. Caroline, who had been trapped in the muck and mire of religiosity, thinking that she could just be a good person and make it into heaven, eventually found out that it had nothing to do with her righteousness and everything to do with His sacrifice. Ian thought that he could give his allegiance to Satan and his life would be paved with his greatest desires, but instead the devil was trying to lead him to an early grave by the strength of his own hand. The apostle Paul, before his radical transformation, thought he was serving God while actually doing the devil's work.

How do we avoid such confusion? We understand that all that we need to live a life of godliness in Christ Jesus is already written. We understand that we have to take part in the process and do our part for kingdom expansion. We understand that time is short and there is a real urgency. The battle for souls is fought in the heavenlies; every time you or I share the gospel, every time we lift a loved one's name before the throne of grace, and every time we invite someone to church, we are helping someone else find the abundant life Jesus came to give us. We have to be diligent to set our own standard of living by God's standards, not the standards set by ourselves or society. The most critical aspect of living a rich life is based on the decision to follow Jesus Christ, to accept him as Lord and Savior, and to know beyond a shadow of doubt that there is a life after this life in eternity. As Frederick Robertson once said, "In these two things the greatness of man consists. One is to have God so dwelling in us as to impart His character to us; and the other is to have God so dwelling in us that we recognize His presence, and know that we are His and He is ours. They are two things perfectly distinct. To have God in us, this is salvation; to know that God is in us, this is assurance."[6]

How do you weigh your own righteousness? Abundant living starts with Jesus Christ, and it ends with Jesus Christ, and every moment in between is precious as we serve our living Savior. Take this free gift of salvation and share the good news, and begin your journey to a life well lived.

Intentional Living

- Salvation is the first step in living a life of no regrets.
- Share your life's story; it can open hearts to receive the truth.
- Share your faith whenever you can; the rewards are eternal.
- Acknowledge the absolutes found in Scripture and live by them regardless of what society says.
- Judge your righteousness by God's standard, not by the world's standards.
- A true God-encounter will always result in a changed life.
- Impactful living is living for Christ no matter your circumstances.

CHAPTER 3

REFINEMENT: A TEST AND PURIFICATION OF THE HEART

Love loves unto purity. Love has ever in view the absolute loveliness of that which it beholds. Therefore all that is not beautiful in the beloved, all that comes between and is not of love's kind, must be destroyed. And our God is a consuming fire.

—GEORGE MACDONALD[1]

WHAT IF THIS were your last day on this earth? If you were going to stand before God tomorrow, what would you change today? I asked my husband this question. He said, "I'd forgive more. I would make things right in all my relationships. I would ask to be forgiven."

I said, "Then why wait?" Why not do what you know to do today instead of waiting until you are pressured into making changes or have to suffer greatly for refusing to make those changes? We all do it. We all know the right things to do. We all put things off for another day or perhaps a more opportune time. I thought, "What would I be willing to change?" I will share my answer shortly.

God changes us if we fail to make the changes that we should make:

And it will happen in all the land, says the LORD, that two-thirds will be cut off and die, and one-third will be left in the land. And I will bring this one-third left into the fire, and will refine them as the refinement of silver, and will test them as the testing of gold. They will call on My name, and I will answer them. I will say, "They are My people"; and they will say, "The LORD is my God."

—ZECHARIAH 13:8–9

God changes us if we fail to make the changes that we should make, and sometimes we are refined so that we are cleansed of the very things that hold us back from our destiny. He refines us. Refinement is a hard process.

Silver was discovered around 4000 BC and became a medium of exchange as well as being used to make jewelry. Two thousand years later mining and silver smelting was underway. Silver-bearing ores are often found mixed with copper, lead, or zinc. During the refining process the silver gets stripped away from the other minerals, heated in a furnace, and cleansed of all its impurities.

Refinement is a hard process for us as well, but the finished work is a beautiful reflection of Christ shining through us. As believers we reflect Christ best when our flesh is out of the way and when we have been purged of the things that defile. As we are refined, we move from glory to glory, becoming more like Christ in our actions and our thinking. Our lives become lives that are not so cluttered with regret because we live intentionally with the goal of pleasing God first in mind. Our life experience is richer and deeper because of our enhanced understanding of God, our greater trust in God, and our complete dependence on God. How do you get started? By starting today and choosing to live as if this was going to be your last day on the earth. That is sound advice from someone who knows what it actually feels like to face the real possibility of an early death. How would you live today if you knew you would stand before God tomorrow?

Pillar of Abundant Living

In this you greatly rejoice, even though now, if for a little while, you have had to suffer various trials, in order that the genuineness of your faith, which is more precious than gold that perishes, though it is tried by fire, may be found to result in praise, glory, and honor at the revelation of Jesus Christ.

—1 Peter 1:6–7

What is at the end of a time of refinement? Let's look for one moment at the end before the beginning. Joy is at the end of the refinement. Let me say that again: joy is at the end of our refinement. That is why James, the brother of Jesus, could write, "Count it all joy," and Paul could echo the sentiment (James 1:2; Phil. 1:20–21). They knew we would, after going through a process of refinement, come out stronger, more patient, more content, and more confident in the Lord. They knew that we would come out on the other side reflecting more of God: more of His love, more of His mercy, more of His compassion, and more of His grace.

BIRTHING PAINS

My husband and I were walking by a large pond in our neighborhood. We live in the Low Country of South Carolina, and our ponds are full of alligators as well as other reptiles and amphibians. We also have blue herons, snowy egrets, cormorants, ospreys, red-tailed hawks, ibis, and wood storks, all of which make our walks so incredibly delightful. That day the gators were out in full force. We must have seen five or six on our short walk. For the first time ever we heard an alligator growl. Our neighbors, who were walking several steps ahead, stopped and shouted back, "Hey, did you hear that?"

"Yes," I said, "but what is it?" Our neighbor replied that it was the sound of an alligator in mating season.

It reminded me of a time when I was a young woman, and I growled at my husband in that same way. It was in the labor room as I was getting ready to give birth to my son. I had been in hard, Pitocin-induced labor, with its characteristic intense and abrupt contractions of the uterus, for eighteen hours. I cannot remember ever being in such pain. It seemed as though it would go on forever. However, when my sweet baby son was placed in my arms, all the pain I experienced seemed to fade from my memory. As I peered into his beautiful blue eyes, I saw in him the reflection of my husband and me looking down at him. Joy. What joy. He was perfect.

When a baby is being born, it has to be pushed through the birth canal. He has to leave his place of security and comfort and go to a new place, a place of the unknown. It cannot be a pain-free process for either the mother or the child, but when complete, the baby feels safe in his parents' arms. The child quickly identifies with the mother who carried him for nine months, and then recognizes the father as he quickly connects with him also. The pain is soon forgotten, and the joy of new life takes its place.

If you have ever had children, you might remember that precious look in your babies' eyes when they first looked up and recognized their father. The newborn knows almost nothing, yet he knows to whom he belongs. Think back to the time when you saw the father gazing into the eyes of his newborn. Dad was beaming with joy at every sound and every little movement.

Now take this picture of a father and a newborn and apply that to how God feels when we have come through a difficult period of refinement. He smiles down at His child. He is so pleased. He sees more of His own perfect reflection as He gazes into the soul that has been refined. Was all the pain worth it? Yes. Yes. Yes. Pain is here for a time, but joy comes in the morning after the darkness of the night. Joy bubbles up on the inside of you when you come through the fires of refinement. It is a joy that cannot compare with mere happiness. It's deeper. It's richer. It's more intense. It is a joy that cannot be shaken.

As you enter periods of refinement, try to remember the principle A. W. Tozer points out so eloquently: "He remembers our frame and knows that we are dust. He may sometimes chasten us, it is true, but even this He does with a smile, the proud, tender smile of a Father who is bursting with pleasure over an imperfect but promising son who is coming every day to look more and more like the One whose child he is." [2]

REFLECTIONS

God sees Himself in the eyes of the refined soul. Embrace refinement. Remember what happens to you when you get through it. You've heard the old cliché: "Don't get bitter; get better." The getting better part is the very purpose of refinement. It is not punishment. It is tough love.

Discipline is the result of something we have done while refinement is the preparation for your calling. God disciplines us when we refuse to obey, not to punish us but instead to teach us. God refines us by showing us what is really in our hearts and then removing all that is not like Him so that we will better reflect His goodness. Both refinement and discipline are actions that God will use to get us to become all that we are to become for His glory. For example, a father will discipline a child for not cleaning his room by taking away a privilege. A father may refine his child by going into his room with him, looking under the bed, looking in the closet, and cleaning it up with him. Thus, the testing part: "How clean is the room really, son? Let's take a look together, and I will help you get things in order."

We know that God disciplines those whom He loves (Heb. 12:6). Discipline is a loving way to get you back on track with God. Refinement is a loving way to empty you of all that is not like Him, fill you with more of Him, and prepare you for the work ahead. God always wants to move us from glory to glory, but to get to the next level of glory, He must take us through the fires of refinement, especially if there are things in us that are not reflective of Him. If we fail to deal with those things, He will deal with them.

When I went through the fires of refinement, I asked myself and God many questions. "Am I being sifted? Am I being disciplined? Am I being punished? God, what are You doing to me? God, are You going to let me be destroyed?"

THE WHAT

A refiner's fire is the process that we go through when God is testing us to see what is in our hearts. The change in us comes when we acknowledge there needs to be a change. However, it is not punishment; it is testing, and then the purging begins. Job wrote that although God knew the way he would take when He tested him, he would come out like gold (Job 23:10). Job had to know in his own heart if he was serving God for what He had done for him, or if he was serving God for who God is alone, regardless of what He had done. Job had to know that he would serve God no matter what circumstances he was in. Sometimes we are not sure in our own hearts, so refinement is necessary. God tested the Israelites in the desert. He tested them so that they would know what was in their own hearts. God already knew. He wanted them to know, and He wants us to know also. A faith that is not tested is not a genuine faith.

Trials come. Tribulation comes. Fires of refinement come. The purpose of refinement is to bring to light the things hidden in darkness and then remove them. After the testing, the purging will begin. However, as believers we are to count it all joy when we have to face various trials and temptations (James 1:2). How can we do that? Are we supposed to fake our way through it? Are we to put on a happy face when everything in us is hurting? I think our real test is to not become a victim of our own circumstances but instead to be victorious knowing that through the trial we are being refined. We are being purged of all that is not like God.

And this is an important process. After all, as Charles Spurgeon once said, "No faith is so precious as that which lives and triumphs in adversity. Tried faith brings experience. You could not have believed your own weakness had you not been compelled to pass through the rivers; and you would never have known God's strength had you not been supported amid the water-floods."[3]

THE WHY

We are a rebellious people, stiff-necked and often hardheaded. However, God will not allow us to stay in that condition. Our hearts are deceitfully wicked; even the most righteous cannot match the perfect righteousness of Jesus Christ. He is our standard of measurement. He will allow us to be tested, or He Himself will test us. He will test us, but He will never tempt us. The Lord said in the Book of Jeremiah, "Now, I will refine them and assay them; for what else shall I do for the daughter of My people?" (Jer. 9:7). You can almost hear the frustration in His voice.

Testing will prove to be effective in exposing our heart motives, humbling us, and determining whether or not we will actually obey His commands (Deut. 8:2). Have you ever been tested or been through the fires of refinement? I have, and it is not easy. At what point in your life, if ever, would you curse God, deny God, or turn from God? At what point would you declare that you were never going to serve God again? Think about the life of Job.

Job was tested not because he was unrighteous but because he was righteous. Not all fires are the result of disobedience. Refiner's fires are to take us to the next level of godliness. Some fires are to ensure that we, when stripped of everything, are not serving God for what He can do for us but for who He is. Satan was looking for one whom he could sift, and God suggested Job.

"What? Are you kidding me?" That is what I used to think. I struggled with the thought that God would suggest that His righteous servant be tested. Job's wife was angry and told him to curse God and die. His friends told him to confess his hidden sins because he must have been in sin. And everyone around thought God had abandoned him. But did God abandon him? Absolutely not! Job lost everything. He lost his children. He lost his property. He lost many friends. He even lost his health. Yet in the midst of his trials, Job was never abandoned by God. God knew what Job would do. Satan did not. Satan declared that Job would fall if God removed His hand of protection from him. God knew, however, that Job would bring Him glory by refusing to allow the circumstances around him to overthrow his faith in the only true God.

The pain of refinement is real. Look at Job. Job passed his test, and God was greatly glorified. Job was a man who loved the Lord. He was righteous; God described him as "a blameless and an upright man, who fears God, and avoids evil" (Job 1:8). He was successful and honorable, but God turned him over to be sifted. "Job, if I take everything, will you still love Me?" God did not say those words to him, but that's how I see the story playing out. Sifting, burning, and purging: all have the same intended purpose. "What will you do if I remove My hand of blessing from your life?" Job lost almost everything and everyone through the process.

The fires of refinement will shine the light of Christ into the dark places of our hearts, burn off the chaff, and restore us to a state of greater purity. They will bring to light the things hidden in darkness and then remove them. Peter was sifted. The fire was hot. The mob was angry. The crucifixion was hours away. Peter said he would not deny Jesus, yet in the midst of the heat he did. In a moment of fear and temptation he gave in to his circumstances and refused to even acknowledge knowing Jesus (Luke 22:57). However, through his failure, something in Peter changed. Through that time of testing, although he failed, he gained the strength and ability to stand for Christ again and even die for him.

How many times have we done the very same thing? We deny Jesus by our words, by our deeds, or by our neglect. We wonder how it was possible for Peter to do such a thing when he walked with Jesus day after day. Truth be told, we have been guilty of doing the very same thing. God forgive us! Jesus knew Peter would deny Him, but He also knew that when the time came, Peter would be willing to give up his life for the cause of Christ. Why do we go through a refiner's fire? The Lord tests our hearts, not for His knowledge or benefit but for ours. He already knows what is in our hearts. He tests our hearts so that *we* may know what is truly in our own hearts.

Pillar of Abundant Living

The crucible is for silver, and the furnace is for gold, and the LORD tests hearts.

—Proverbs 17:3, ESV

A number of years ago while living in North Carolina, I was experiencing a day like any other day, doing some computer work and sitting outside by my pool. A woman who I had been teaching in one of my Bible classes called. Her husband had been arrested and accused of atrocious acts. She screamed over the phone, "If God lets this happen, I will never serve or honor Him again. Why would God allow something like this to happen when we have been serving Him?" This woman loved the Lord, but her life was falling apart and there was nothing she could do. I said, "If ever there is a time you need God, it is now. Do not cut off the only One who can help you and your family out of this devastation." This was a time of intense testing. Believe me, the fire was hot. People assume things. People talk. Reputations are ruined.

Why would God allow a family to go through such a difficult time? With Job, with Peter, and with the Israelites God wanted them to know what was in their own hearts. He will test our faith. He will throw it all up in the air with the chaff and see what is left on the ground and what blows away with the wind (sifting like wheat). This woman's circumstances were a perfect example of a refiner's fire. It was a time when God was using this family as an instrument of His glory. It was a time to examine what decisions they would make in the midst of tremendous injustice. God could have asked, "Will you praise Me in the pit?" He could have asked, "Will you love Me when all has been stripped away? Will you love Me when life didn't turn out the way you wanted it to turn out?" What would you do if God chose to not give you the answers you wanted, the healing you prayed for, the salvation of that wayward child, or the restoration of a terrible marriage? What would you do?

Pillar of Abundant Living

For You, O God, have proved us; You have refined us, as silver is refined....We went through fire and through water; but You brought us out into a well-watered place.
—Psalm 66:10-12

THE HOW

The method often used for refining is the experience of intense struggles or trials that come out of the blue. It can be your health, your reputation, your family, your career, or your relationships being attacked or compromised in some way. These struggles just pop up unexpectedly out of nowhere. They hardly make any sense when they appear. They are supernatural in nature. You cannot stop, redirect, or change them. You are totally and completely dependent on God and have no way of controlling the outcome. What would you do? What would you do if God lifted His hand of protection as He did with Job and let you be sifted like wheat? The act of refining will take something in its current state and, through certain processes, remove the impurities from the original substance. Refinement makes it more usable, frees it of all impurities, and renders it in its purest form. The fires of refinement are just the first part, then afterward the purging will begin to remove the dross or impurities. We go through a cleansing from the impurities that are in our hearts so that we can better reflect Christ.

In the Fire

We as believers know that every word of God is flawless. The Bible clearly teaches that God is a shield to those who take refuge in Him (Ps. 18:30). When we are being refined, it seems like everything in this world is going wrong. It seems like everything is caving in around us, and it can feel very hot. But hear me: you can survive regardless of the trial; and not only can you survive, but you can also thrive and expect to come out on the other side with joy, being restored and strengthened in God. Now that we know what the fires of refinement are, how do we get through them?

The Word

The Word says, "Every word of God is pure; He is a shield to those who put their trust in Him" (Prov. 30:5). Do you hear that? He is a shield to those who trust Him. In the midst of refinement you have to take refuge in God, in His Word, and in His promises, and you have to stand firm. This is a time when you have to declare the Word of God over your situation and believe it. When I had a death sentence hanging over my head, I had to war for my health by declaring His promises and believing them without doubt, without wavering, and without fear. God was gracious to me.

Humility before His holiness

Out of the fires of refinement come the praise of His magnificence, the brilliance of His glory, and the honor of His precious Son, Jesus Christ. I can promise you this: during a time of refinement, you will either be angry with God and blame Him, or you will fall on your knees, worship Him, and plead for mercy. God acknowledges those who humble themselves. He hears the cries of His people.

Intensity of the prayer

My prayer life intensified, and yours will too when you are in a time of refinement. My prayer life became focused, unrelenting, and specific. It was a time of deep introspection and honesty with myself and with God. I fell on my knees night after night and cried out to Him. I begged. I pleaded. I wept. I confessed. I needed Him, and I knew that it would mean total surrender.

Shareworthy

A man by his sin may waste himself, which is to waste that which on earth is most like God. This is man's greatest tragedy and God's heaviest grief.

—A. W. Tozer[4]

Confession and repentance

The fires of refinement will not destroy you, but the sin in which you are entangled may. God will at times use the fires of refinement to bring sin to an end in your heart. For me it was a time of confession and repentance. You will repent of things you are not even sure you've done, just in case. Daniel 11:35 speaks of this in the last days: "Some of the wise will fall, so that they may be purged, purified, and made white, until the time of the end, for it is still for the appointed time."

Faith

Genuine faith breaks forth from the iron smelter of affliction. God is pleased when you respond in faith as you face these trials. How do I know that for certain? Because the Bible says that without faith it is impossible to please God (Heb. 11:6). Faith is believing in Jesus and all that He said and taught. It is that faith that overcomes the world and the things of this world. As Galatians 2:20 says, you have been crucified with Christ; it is not your life you live, but the life of Christ shining forth from you.

PURITY

The ultimate purpose of the fires of refinement is the purification that we gain through the process. Remember, while in the fires of refinement you should get into the Word, humble yourself, intensify your prayer life, confess your sins, repent and turn from your sins, act in faith, and trust that God is purifying you.

PILLAR OF ABUNDANT LIVING

Consider how much love the Father has given to us, that we should be called children of God. Therefore the world does not know us, because it did not know Him. Beloved, now are we children of God, and it has not yet been revealed what we shall be. But we know that when He appears, we shall be like Him, for we shall see Him as He is. Everyone who has this hope in Him purifies himself, just as He is pure.

—1 John 3:1–3

BENEFITS OF REFINEMENT

What came out of that furnace of affliction? What benefits did the people of God attain? What happened to the enemy who tried to destroy them? Well, Job received back double for his trouble. Peter became a man on a mission where even the fear of dying for that mission had been conquered. It was because of his time of sifting that he became that overcomer. Israel became a nation again, and God's hand will always be her protector. And they all were victorious over the enemy who tried to destroy them.

Pillar of Abundant Living

But we all, seeing the glory of the Lord with unveiled faces, as in a mirror, are being transformed into the same image from glory to glory by the Spirit of the Lord.

—2 Corinthians 3:18

Though the fire and water tried to overtake me, I came out to a place of great abundance. I know that the fires of refinement, although hard, dark, and difficult, brought me to a better and richer place in God. I know that God has restored me, strengthened me, comforted me, and established me. The refining work is the work of the Holy Spirit. God, through the work of the Holy Spirit, does the purifying work in us. We just have to be willing to do it God's way as we are going through the process.

Shareworthy

The furnace of trouble is often used as a mode of refining, but after all it is only a means; the real refining fire is the Holy Ghost, the true purification...

—Charles Spurgeon[5]

The fires of refinement come with a cost but also with a promise. His grace has been extended forth to you for restoration, comfort, strengthening, and establishment in Him. You will be restored. You will be strengthened. You will be comforted. You will be established. Through the testing of your faith you will gain greater endurance, and that endurance, when perfected, will bring you to a place of being complete, lacking nothing. Endurance, perseverance, patience, and greater faith will all bring glory to God, which is more valuable than silver or gold. You will either choose the fires of refinement or the fires of affliction by default. Refinement happens so that you and I can bear more of His image. We are purged of those hidden sins. We understand with greater clarity how precious every moment we've been given is.

A Changed Life

I went out to lunch with a friend who has a husband facing serious health issues. She said, "Robin, he has changed. I walked by him the other day and he said, 'Honey, I love you.' It had been quite a while since he had used those words."

I said, "Katherine, what if he realized how much he appreciated you all those many years ago? How would your life, your family, and your children be different today?"

How did I change my life during my refining process? I refused to hold my husband hostage for his shortcomings. I forgave family members who had repeatedly hurt, rejected, or attacked me without cause. I decided my days would be filled with good thoughts rather than worry and regret. My thoughts would be filled with the Word of God and joyous memories, and I made a point to treasure each and every moment. I tell people I love them more frequently. I laugh a lot more. I enjoy the beauty that surrounds me. My plan is to serve God to the best of my ability every day of my life. Will this way of living wear off? No way. I have been given a second chance, a chance to enjoy this life with all the precious things it has to give. I have learned to take one day at a time because I realize I have no promise of tomorrow.

You might ask, "Have others changed toward you?" Some have. Some have not. Regardless, I have changed, and I thank God every day for the newness of spirit, my revival, He has given me. We are tested; through that testing we gain endurance, and through that endurance, as we allow it to have its perfect result, we ourselves become complete, lacking nothing. It is by our endurance that we win life. It is by endurance that we gain our very souls. So what are the results of the fires of refinement? Joy, joy, joy. Refinement results in greater patience and endurance, greater love, greater appreciation of people, and most importantly a greater appreciation for God.

When trials come, when the heat is turned up and all looks lost, remember the kindness of God and His gracious restoration, and rejoice in the fires of refinement. Good is on the way.

Intentional Living

- Do not run away from refinement. It's not punishment; it is preparation.
- Remember, the purpose of refinement is to bring to light the things hidden in darkness and then remove them; embrace the opportunity.
- Know that faith that is tested and proven true will help you to become a person who can influence and impact others for the better.
- After the process of refinement, expect to find increased joy and an unshakable spirit.
- Refinement will help to remove those things in life that cause our deepest regrets; let this happen.
- Allow the fires of refinement to shine the light of Christ into the dark places of your heart, burn off the chaff, and move you to a state of greater purity.
- Know that through refinement His grace has been given to you for restoration, comfort, and strengthening, which will help you better reflect Christ.

PART II

LIVE A LEGACY

CHAPTER 4

THE POWER OF PRAYER

Is it not sweet to believe that our tears are understood even when words fail? Let us learn to think
of tears as liquid prayers, and of weeping as a constant dropping of importunate intercession which will
wear its way right surely into the very heart of mercy,
despite the stony difficulties which obstruct the way.

—CHARLES SPURGEON [1]

IT WAS A cold winter's night in the mountains of Alleghany
County, Virginia, when I, at the age of seventeen, needed an
answered prayer in the worst way. I was on my way home from
a football game, and a friend of mine needed a ride. I told her I
would be happy to take her home. The roads were starting to get
icy; there was no snow yet, but you could feel the temperature had
dropped pretty significantly. We made it to her home without an
issue; however, as I was heading home myself, I hit a patch of ice and
the car started to drift off of the road. My wheels were spinning, but
I was not going forward. Instead my car was sliding sideways. On
the right side of the road was a steep cliff, and below the cliff was a
cold, icy, rushing river. It all happened so quickly, though it felt as
if time stood still. My heart was pounding in my chest. I thought I
was going to die. My car was heading right for the edge of that cliff,
and my steering wheel was completely useless. As I was nearing the
edge, I cried out, "God, please save me!" As the words were leaving
my mouth, I felt something supernatural. It's hard to explain, but
it felt as though a hand picked up the back end of my car and set
it right back on the road. If you've ever had a near miss, then you
know exactly what I am talking about. I remember that night so
vividly because I feel certain that without the help of the Lord, I
would have been dead. God has a purpose for my life, and He, and
He alone, is my protector.

My life would follow a pattern. Year after year I found myself in situations through which only God could help me. I learned at an early age to lean on Him and that He would be there with me. As Psalms says, "Then they cried out to the Lord in their trouble, and He saved them out of their distress. He made the storm calm, and the sea waves were still. They were glad because the waters were quiet, so He brought them to their desired harbor" (Ps. 107:28–30).

Do you want to live a life of no regrets? Do you want to make good and right decisions in your life? Do you want to know what your assignments are? Then you need to know how to pray, and you need to know that the prayers you pray will be heard and answered. Prayer is a tool that God grants so that we can learn how best to reflect Him, becoming more like Him as we grow to better know Him. It is an action based on a simple belief that God can and will bring about change in the course of events. It is communication with an expectation that God will lead us and that He will hear and answer. Expect nothing less than answered prayers. Oftentimes we will pray a prayer but not expect to get an answer. That's futile. The Word of God tells us to come boldly to the throne of grace (Heb. 4:16). Prayer should be your first defense, not your last resort. Prayer will help you live a life with no regrets because through prayer you learn to follow the lead of the Lord. Through prayer, if prayed confidently in faith, God will bring about direction, conviction, clarification, inspiration, and revelation, and He will give you wisdom to make decisions that will help you live the best life you can live.

Light Sown

We often hear of seeds sown as representative of a financial offering, but did you know that light has been sown like seed for the righteous? Psalm 97:11 talks of this: "Light is sown like seed for the righteous and gladness for the upright in heart" (NASB). Does this make your heart rejoice? It does mine. I am constantly amazed at the goodness of God. Light sown like seeds tells me that a glimmer of direction and guidance is already in place, and it will come into being at just the right time. When the time comes, that which has been sown will come forth; the very light that I need to see will be awaiting me. I do not know about you, but I am constantly seeking God for direction and help. I need Him, and I can say with certainty that you need Him too. We need to see where we are going as well as which path to walk on.

One afternoon years ago, I was taking an SUV full of children to the zoo in Jacksonville, Florida. We were all excited to spend the day having fun on our outing. I stopped to fill my vehicle up with gasoline, and I was directed by the Holy Spirit to pray over the vehicle. Please hear me—this was not the typical pray-before-you-travel prayer. I was overwhelmed in my spirit with an urgent need for warfare prayer. I knew in my spirit that this was direction from the Lord, so I prayed fervently. We traveled to Jacksonville from southeast Georgia, spent the day, and were on our way back home when a Mack truck pulled out right in front of me. Another vehicle was practically at a stop on the interstate in front of me. I had no place to go. Now I do not know if you are a believer in supernatural intervention, but I want you to know that God spared me and a whole SUV filled with children. I will never forget that moment. It was as though the hand of God opened a path just wide enough for me to pass safely through. Our lives were spared that day.

At the end of the day I was so very thankful for the light that had been sown for me. Light sown that showed me my need for urgent prayer. Light sown that showed me there was danger ahead. Light sown that showed a narrow path of escape. I am forever thankful for light, which has been sown like seed for the righteous. Our God is a great and mighty God. He reigns, and He deserves all of our love, our adoration, and our devotion. Prayer is, in a word, intimacy that we have to choose to pursue. There is great power in prayer that is led of the Holy Spirit; when you've been led to pray by the power of the Holy Spirit, the victory is already yours. Do not doubt, but rejoice in the victory that awaits you.

PRIORITIES

After my trip to Italy I was supposed to get to my doctor as quickly as possible. However, I could not get in for months, so I called the

Mayo Clinic on my own. After hearing my symptoms, the nurse did a rare thing. She went to the chief doctor on staff that day to explain my symptoms, and they made an appointment for me to come in without a referral—something they never do. It was God. However, I had already decided I was going to the church to be prayed over first with *the prayer of faith.* I wanted to put my healing in the hands of God rather than the hands of the doctors. Hear me: I know that God gives doctors wisdom to bring about healing, but I also know that it is God who does the healing. After the elders of the church prayed for me, it was time for me to do my own praying. Herein lies the importance of intimacy. Thankfully by this time in my life I had been accustomed to praying to God for everything. This incident would be no different. It was, however, a matter of life and death. I needed God again, and my life depended on it.

As I mentioned, prayer should be your first defense; prayer should be where you go first, not where you go as a last resort. You will pray with faith, or you will pray from a position of doubt; only one way honors God and gives Him reason to move in your situation. Without faith it is impossible to please God. He rewards those who earnestly seek Him.

THE PRAYER OF FAITH

The Book of James teaches us about the prayer of faith: "Is anyone sick among you? Let him call for the elders of the church, and let them pray over him, anointing him with oil in the name of the Lord. And the prayer of faith will save the sick, and the Lord will raise him up. And if he has committed any sins, he will be forgiven. Confess your faults to one another and pray for one another, that you may be healed. The effective, fervent prayer of a righteous man accomplishes much" (5:14–16).

Prayer without faith is as futile as a body without breath. Faith is the instrument used to propel our prayers into the ears and heart of God. The Bible reads, "Without faith it is impossible to please God" (Heb. 11:6). In the scripture from James we see that the prayer of faith is for those who are sick as well as those trapped in sin. The *prayer of faith* is prayed by the elders of a church; they anoint the individual seeking prayer with oil and pray over him or her for healing if it is a physical issue or for forgiveness if it is a sin issue. The prayer, accompanied by anointing with oil, is offered in the name of the Lord. The power is in His name, not in the words or the oil. It is prayed in faith with all confidence that God can and will heal. It is His name, His Word, and His character to heal. Does God always heal? No. Is it because of lack of faith? At times it may be due to lack of faith, but more often I think it is simply a mystery we will only understand when we get to heaven. We have to be OK with that. Some live; some die. Does that mean we should not pray the *prayer of faith* in case it doesn't work? Absolutely not. Prayer is made in full confidence of God's power to heal because it is His name and His character (Exod. 15:26; 23:25; Deut. 7:15); *Jehovah Rapha*, the God who heals you, is one of God's names. We should pray with complete expectation that our prayers will be answered. I thank God that I took Him at His Word and prayed this prayer.

Pillar of Abundant Living

O LORD my God, I cried out to You, and You healed me.

—Psalm 30:2

The prayer of faith is the church displaying the manifold wisdom, power, and greatness of God (Eph. 3:10), and it comes with a promise attached: the Lord will raise them up. It is for those who are sick, that they may be healed, and it is for the sinners, that they will be forgiven. This prayer is for the church; God is giving clear instruction on what we are to do. It is for those who intercede, as an exercise of their faith. Their prayers are powerful and effective because of faith in His name and the biblical precedent for the prayer. The prayer of faith is for today. If we think that Jesus went about doing good and taught His disciples to do the same but for some strange reason ended that good after His resurrection, then we have faith that is in vain. The same Spirit that raised Christ from the dead is living in us (Rom. 8:11).

Shareworthy

"With all prayer (Eph. 6:18)" All sorts of prayer—public, private, mental, vocal. Do not be diligent in one kind of prayer and negligent in others...let us use all.

—John Wesley [2]

THE PRAYER OF AGREEMENT

Agree with God. Agree with Satan. Agree with your flesh. Whichever choice you make, there is only one decision that works in your best interest. The Bible clearly shows that there is great power in the prayer of agreement: "Again I say to you, that if two of you agree on earth about anything they ask, it will be done for them by My Father who is in heaven" (Matt. 18:19).

The prayer of agreement is when you first come into agreement with God and then with another saint of God who joins in the petition and understands the concept of the prayer of agreement.

I had a dear friend, Jewel, who was on the verge of losing her home. We joined our hearts in faith and believed God would intervene in the situation. Her husband had been sick and lost his job, and because of the cost of their medical bills they could not pay their house payments. They were going to have to put the house on the market. One day Jewel went into her business and a client came in. Jewel was quite disturbed and clearly stressed, so her client asked her what was going on. Jewel explained that she was going to have to sell her home. Her client told Jewel to meet her on the following Monday. That Monday the two met and the dear woman put a check in Jewel's hand for the total amount due on her home, one hundred eighty thousand dollars. The client wasn't buying the home from her; she was paying it off for her. Who does that? Jewel called me that day, and we cried. It was not God's will for these saints of God to lose their home. We cried with joy. We cried because God is so faithful. We cried because He has so much love for His children. We cried because He heard our prayer of agreement and graciously decided to answer it.

THE PRAYER OF DEDICATION

We are to dedicate our children, our homes, our firstfruits, our work, and even our own bodies as living sacrifices unto the Lord. Dedication sets something apart for sacred use. God gives to us, and we give back to Him. He takes what is ordinary, and it becomes extraordinary. Read about the prayer of dedication Hannah prayed for her son:

> And she said, "Oh, my lord! As you live, my lord, I am the woman that stood by you here praying to the LORD. For this boy I prayed, and the LORD has given me my petition which I asked of Him. Therefore also I have let the LORD have him. As long as he lives he will be dedicated to the LORD." And [Eli] worshiped the LORD there.
>
> —1 SAMUEL 1:26–28

We are most familiar with baby dedications. Children are a gift from God, and they belong first and foremost to Him. Baby dedication is an opportunity for believing parents, and sometimes entire families, to make a commitment before the Lord to submit a child to God's will and to raise that child according to God's Word and God's ways. Hannah prayed for a baby, and the Lord heard her and answered her prayers. She then, in turn, sacrificially gave her baby, Samuel, back to God, sanctified for His service. Are there things in your life right now that you should dedicate to the Lord?

THE PRAYER OF THANKSGIVING

The Psalms are filled with prayers of thanksgiving to God. Here is one of many: "I face your holy Temple, bow down, and praise your name because of your constant love and faithfulness, because you have shown that your name and your commands are supreme. You answered me when I called to you; with your strength you strengthened me." (Ps. 138:2–3, GNT).

Prayer and thanksgiving go hand in hand. We know that Jesus, when He broke bread, gave thanks to His heavenly Father (Luke 22:19). We know that Paul taught we are to pray with thanksgiving. The psalmist prayed, "I thank you, LORD, with all my heart" (Ps. 138:1, GNT). There is clear precedent throughout Scripture that thanksgiving is an important aspect and attitude of prayer.

Shareworthy

God is intricately involved in our lives, and for that alone we should be thankful.

—Robin Bertram

Well-known theologian John Wesley once said, "Thanksgiving is inseparable from true prayer; it is almost essentially connected with it. One who always prays is ever giving praise, whether in ease or pain, both for prosperity and for the greatest adversity. He blesses God for all things, looks on them as coming from Him, and receives them for His sake—not choosing nor refusing, liking nor disliking, anything, but only as it is agreeable or disagreeable to His perfect will."[3]

The *prayer of thanksgiving* is a prayer, or a portion of a prayer, that thanks God for who He is, what He has done, and what He will do. God is omniscient, omnipresent, and omnipotent; He knows all things, He is ever present, and He is all-powerful. God is intricately involved in our lives, and for that alone we should be thankful. Have you ever given something to your children and they did not say thank you or even acknowledge your kind act toward them? Did you feel like taking the gift back? Most likely you did, especially if it was a costly gift. Our salvation cost God everything. Gratitude in our hearts shows God the appreciation He well deserves.

THE PRAYER OF INTERCESSION

We know that there is one mediator between God and man, and that mediator is Jesus Christ. We are, however, to pray and intercede on behalf of all men: leaders, those in authority over us, and those in need. Paul discussed this in a letter: "I exhort first of all that you make supplications, prayers, intercessions, and thanksgivings for everyone" (1 Tim. 2:1).

Several years ago a friend asked me to pray for a young man named Nathan whose life was in transition; that was all the information that was given. I prayed that day for the young man, and then in the middle of that night I sat straight up in bed. The Lord had given me a vision of two slit wrists. My knees hit the floor. I cried out to God. "No, God. No. Please intervene. Please prevent this from happening." I stayed up most of the rest of that night crying out to God. Tuesday morning I got a call from my friend. We exchanged pleasantries and then she asked, "Did you get an opportunity to pray for Nathan?"

"Yes, I did," I replied. "Can you tell me if he is suicidal?"

My friend started to cry, "How did you know?" I said that God had given me a vision in the middle of the night on Friday. She said that he had been on suicide watch all weekend long, and they were thankful to God that he made it. He was from a very prominent family in Virginia and had been arrested for being with several men who had committed a crime, and now he was facing the possibility of a long-term prison sentence.

I learned from this incident that when God calls you to pray, you pray. I also learned of the great power in intercessory prayer. Again, the power is not in the words; the power comes from a prayer prayed in faith and compassion from the heart. I did not need to know all the details because God knew them. All I needed to do was to be willing to allow God to use me. Would Nathan have lived regardless my prayers? Perhaps. But for me, the indisputable facts were that God prompted my friend to ask me to pray, God gave me the vision of suicide, and then God protected this young man from suicide. What an amazing God we serve! I hope this encourages you to be steadfast in your prayer life. I hope it encourages you to be that intercessor even when things look hopeless. Seemingly hopeless situations are when God's glory usually shines the brightest. We are to come boldly before Him and ask confidently, expecting to receive from Him what He has promised in His Word.

The Prayer of Supplication

E. M. Bounds once said, "Talking to men for God is a great thing, but talking to God for men is greater still. He will never talk well and with real success to men for God who has not learned well how to talk to God for men."[4] Scripture says to "pray in the Spirit always with all kinds of prayer and supplication. To that end be alert with all perseverance and supplication for all the saints" (Eph. 6:18). Supplication is a cry for help that comes from a place of intrinsic desperation resulting from a broken and contrite heart. Supplication is to implore God for mercy and compassion, to have pity on you, or to grant you the request given. When you cry out to Him, you should expect that He will do it. You are in essence asking God with great humility to show favor in a given situation, even in the sense of pleading. Supplication comes from a heart that is passionate about the request and willing to submit to God. Have you ever been desperate? Have you ever been in such great need that only God could grant your request? I've had my back against that wall on numerous occasions. I have no problem pleading for God to grant me mercy when needed, and oftentimes He has.

Shareworthy

Supplication is a cry for help that comes from a place of intrinsic desperation resulting from a broken and contrite heart.

—Robin Bertram

FERVENT, EFFECTUAL PRAYERS

A powerful prayer life is birthed from passion, purpose, and persistence in prayer and is grounded upon biblical precepts of faith, love, and a willingness to obey. Fervent, effectual prayers are passionate prayers of desperation of which God takes note. Hannah prayed for the birth of Samuel. She prayed so fervently that Eli, the priest, accused her of being drunk. He said, "How long will you be drunk? Put away your wine from you" (1 Sam. 1:14). She responded that she was not drunk but pouring her heart out before the Lord. The Word of God goes on to say that she spoke with great anxiety and vexation in supplication. Eli told her to go in peace because God had granted her petition. We are told in Scripture that after hearing him, her countenance was no longer sad (1 Sam. 1:15–18). Because of Hannah's passion, faith, and humility God heard her prayer and granted her request. Hannah displayed faith in her reaction to Eli's word of confirmation. Her entire countenance changed. She also exhibited great love for God in that she was willing to give up the very thing she most treasured, her son, Samuel, by dedicating him to the Lord (1 Sam. 1:26–28).

Fervent, effectual prayers begin with a purpose in mind and end with an answer from God. Yea or nay, either way, you can be sure He heard your requests. If you pray and do not expect an end result, you will not get it. That is for certain. Pray with purpose. Pray with power. Pray with passion. Pray knowing that God is able. As we look at Hannah's prayer, we can see she had an end result in mind—a baby from a barren womb—and He answered her request.

PERSIST IN PRAYER

Shareworthy

Prayer is God's plan to supply man's great and continuous need with God's great and continuous abundance.

—E. M. Bounds [5]

Persistence in prayer is the fuel that feeds a miracle. I am confident that the trip to the tabernacle recorded in 1 Samuel 1 was not Hannah's first prayer to God to ask Him to heal her barren womb and give her a child. The Bible says that Hannah went up year after year and was bitterly provoked by her rival, Peninnah, because she had children, but Hannah had none. Have you ever had someone taunt you because they had something you desperately wanted for your own—children, a good husband, a happy family, a nice home, a prosperous life? Be comforted today. God is still taking note. He is near the brokenhearted; He saves those with a contrite spirit (Ps. 34:18). He knows your pain. The Bible reads that Hannah was greatly distressed, prayed to the Lord, and wept bitterly. Do not give up (Luke 18:1). Keep praying. Persisting in prayer is confidently admitting to the Lord that you have no other alternative, and through your utter helplessness He can and will move. Persisting in prayer allows you to get out of the way.

Pillar of Abundant Living

Ask and it will be given to you; seek and you will find; knock and it will be opened to you.

—Matthew 7:7

Jesus taught His disciples the principle of persistence through a parable of the unjust judge, with Scripture encouraging us "always to pray and not lose heart" (Luke 18:1). He explained that if it were possible for a judge who had no respect for God or man to act on the behalf of this woman because of her persistence, then how much more will God do for those who love Him (Luke 18:1–8). Prayer is a place of total dependence on God where we see our own helplessness as fertile ground for the Lord to plant seeds of faith and love for a fruitful harvest for His kingdom. It is a place of full assurance and confidence that God will accomplish His purposes through us as we reach out to Him with passion, purpose, and persistence.

Be prayerful, and in this you will overcome the regrets of your life and move in greater wisdom and understanding as you submit everything to the Lord. Prayer protects your heart from sin. Prayer opens you up to the leading of the Holy Spirit. Prayer helps to guard you against making poor choices. Prayer helps you to be prepared for good work. There is great power in passionate prayers. Regrets mount when we use poor judgment or make ungodly decisions or connections. God gave us prayer with all its different facets as a beautiful means of communicating with Him so that we can grow in maturity and out of a life filled with regrets. Prayer is a powerful tool.

Shareworthy

It is a sight fit for angels to behold, tears as pearls dropping from a penitent eye!

—Thomas Watson [6]

In Italy I spent nearly every night—all night long—on my face in prayer. I cried out in great desperation. I could not imagine leaving this world early. I could not imagine losing all ability to move on my own. I could not imagine leaving my family behind. I could not imagine not accomplishing the work I know I was sent here to do. My pillow was drenched. I begged. I cried. I pleaded. "God, where are You? God, do You hear me? God, I can't breathe. I can't think. I cannot do this. God, will You please grant this request and let me live?"

He did. And I am eternally grateful.

E. M. Bounds once said, and I have found it to be true, that "God is waiting to be put to the test by His people in prayer. He delights in being put to the test on His promises. It is His highest pleasure to answer prayer, to prove the reliability of His promises."[7]

INTENTIONAL LIVING

- Pray expecting answers.
- Pray knowing God has sown light as seed on your path.
- Pray with unwavering faith that God can do anything.
- Persist in prayer, expecting Him to answer in line with His name, His character, and His Word.
- Pray with sincere thanksgiving for all that He has already done in your life.
- Pray with purpose from a position of victory.
- Pray with passion knowing that God stores up every tear you shed.

CHAPTER 5

AUTHENTIC LOVE

One who has been touched by grace will no longer look
on those who stray as "those evil people" or "those
poor people who need our help." Nor must we search
for signs of "loveworthiness." Grace teaches us that God
loves because of who God is, not because of who we are.

—PHILIP YANCEY[1]

I LOOKED INTO THE eyes of a broken woman: her garments were
tattered, her feet were dirty, and her hair was unkempt. Susan
had a sadness that permeated her very countenance; it could not
be missed. You would most likely not run into her on a Sunday
morning in your church. You could tell life had been very cruel to
her. She had been living in a van with her boyfriend, and they had
parked in the back of another church about four or five miles away
from my church.

The pastor of the church where she and her boyfriend parked
their dilapidated van recommended she come to my church to
receive prayer. The Lord had given me a prayer ministry, and many
people throughout the county came for personal prayer; that is how
I first met Susan. My prayer partner and I prayed for Susan several
times; on her third visit we were instructed by the Holy Spirit to
have a foot-washing ceremony. God had given us eyes of compassion for her. My prayer partner brought out a pan of warm water.
Susan started to cry as her feet went into the water. "Why would
you do this for me? I'm not worthy. I should be doing this for you."
As the tears streamed down her cheeks, I could see the Lord moving
in her heart. It was as if He were saying to her, "You are worthy.
You are My child." Susan gave her life to Jesus. She was healed of a
deep-seated depression and later went on to become a prayer minister herself. If ever there was a time when I tangibly felt the love of

God, it was that very moment when we knelt down to gently wash the feet of a desperate, broken woman.

"Set me as a seal upon your heart, as a seal upon your arm; for love is strong as death, passion fierce as the grave. Its fires of desire are as ardent flames, a most intense flame" (Song of Songs 8:6). Love's flashes are the very flame of the Lord. Love is the deepest expression of God in us because God is love. Love is complex; it is strong; it is weighty. Love is more about what you are willing to give than what you are wanting to get. Love speaks louder than words, and no one has ever demonstrated pure, biblical love better than our Lord and Savior, Jesus Christ. When Jesus walked on this earth, He displayed acts of love for you and me to model, even up to and including His death on the cross. As we model the love walk of Christ, we build a foundation for regret-free living by forging bountiful relationships all around us. And it's through those relationships that we not only enjoy life to the fullest but also create an environment for impacting the lives of others.

Shareworthy

Love is the deepest expression of God in us because God is love.

—Robin Bertram

LOVE DEEPLY

Julian of Norwich once said, "The greatest honor we can give Almighty God is to live gladly because of the knowledge of His love."[2] Living gladly because of His love means loving deeply. If every action, every thought, and every deed were based on and out of the selfless motive of love, then we would most certainly live a life of no regrets. Why? Because we would be reflecting God in us to the fullest extent, and God is love. Love hurts no one. Love manipulates no one. Love mistreats no one. Love damages no one. Love brings only the best to its receiver. Now that is the best way to live a life of no regrets. How can we learn to love more deeply? We all need to learn about loving with greater capacity.

Once we learn what love is, we can learn who we are to love. We are to love God because He first loved us (1 John 4:19). We are to love our neighbors as ourselves (Mark 12:31). We are to love those who hate or despise us. We are to love the most unlovable because that is what Jesus modeled for us. How do we love? We love through the eyes of compassion. We learn to love deeply because that is what Jesus demonstrated for us. This journey that you and I are on is best lived when we follow Jesus's example and teachings and develop our own strong love walk. You will never regret actions done in love or a life filled with an intentional desire to love deeply.

The apostle Paul gave us an incredibly powerful definition of *love* in his letter to the Corinthians, one we can use to help us show His love to those around us:

> Love is patient, love is kind and is not jealous; love does not brag and is not arrogant, does not act unbecomingly; it does not seek its own, is not provoked, does not take into account a wrong suffered, does not rejoice in unrighteousness, but rejoices with the truth; bears all things, believes all things, hopes all things, endures all things. Love never fails.
>
> —1 Corinthians 13:4–8, nasb

What is authentic love? God is love, and love comes from God. Everyone who truly loves has been born of God, and those who do not love, do not know God (1 John 4:7–8). That seems pretty clear-cut to me. However, what is the depth of our love? What is the width of our love? What is the height of our love? We can only begin to understand true love when we understand the love God has for us.

As I was preparing to write this chapter, I stopped in the very beginning and bowed my head to pray. Out of my mouth came this cry: "God, here is yet another bridge I have to cross." God always wants to take us to a new place in Him, a deeper place, a place of greater understanding and dedication. Oftentimes our hearts fool us. We think we are where we need to be. Arrogance of the most deceptive form convinces us that we understand love, that we walk in love, and that we emanate love. However, this is an area of weakness in many people within the body of Christ.

"Robin, how can you possibly say such a thing?" you ask. As I look at those around me, I see poor souls trapped in competition, envy, pride, and jealousy, and then, lo and behold, I see a finger pointed right back to the ugliness of my own heart. We are wretchedly deceived into thinking that we as believers have made it. Day by day, as we peer into the mirror of truth, the Word of God, we should see the frailties of our own human weaknesses. Instead we read it as though it is for another: our spouse, a neighbor, or a friend.

When we look at biblical love, we get a true picture of the need we have in our own hearts to better reflect the love of Christ in a dark and dying world. Love conquers. Love covers. Love endures. Love builds. Love encourages. Love honors. Love suffers. Love believes. It is as strong as death. It is the most powerful force we have in our arsenal for the Lord.

God is love, and if we are to reflect Him, we have to act in love. Love is not a word; it is an action and a deed. It is how we respond to God, to our family and friends, and even to our enemies. It is how we respond to those who are different from us. It is how we respond to those who are unlovable. It is how we respond in our thoughts and in our hearts where no one can see.

WHAT LOVE IS

Authentic biblical love is patient. Love is kind. Love does not envy. Love does not boast. Love is not proud. Stop right there. Have you put your check mark by the first five characteristics of biblical love? Let's look at the characteristics of love found in 1 Corinthians 13 and see if we pass the love test.

Patient

How is your road rage? Is it not your issue? Well, for many years it was mine. I always had to get somewhere: to school to drop off my children, to the grocery store to get dinner, to the bank before it closed, to the hair salon so my stylist would not be angry with me for being five minutes late. There was frequently someone in front of me driving five miles below the speed limit. It's not that I would try to push them out of my way, although I had a rather large GMC Suburban and could have. But I certainly was ready to pass on the solid double lines if given the opportunity. I rushed my way through life more times than I even care to think about.

Although I have been a Christian for most of my life, there were many years when I would have had to place an x by characteristic number one: patience. I would fail at the very first characteristic on the list, and the list becomes even more challenging.

Eventually my road rage was curtailed; one night I was driving home from a television station where I had been asked to speak as a guest on an evening show. I was three hours from home, and it was late. I was tired and speeding home. I was pulled over and given a ticket, not just once, but twice in the same night. God knows just how to bring us back in line, doesn't He? We just have to recognize when it is truly the Lord. I have since then been healed of road rage.

Kind

Authentic biblical love is kind. Do you actively seek ways to be a benefit in the lives of other people? Do you go out of your way to show simple kindness? Do you speak with gentleness in your voice, or are you always yelling the next command to those around you? Kindness that is genuine will warm hearts, bring smiles, and show honor. Spread the joy and be kind.

Recently my husband and I went on a trip, and we had a woman from our church dog-sit our Yorkie, Sophie, for us. When we returned home, everything had been taken care of: the beds stripped, the laundry finished, and the dishes put away. Amanda had gone above and beyond the call of duty. I said to my husband, "If more Christians were like Amanda, we would have a lot more people in heaven." Kindness goes a long way. Kindness can immediately change the atmosphere. It will change the way people respond to you and make your own heart glad. This underrated concept has the power to affect the lives of those around you as well as your own heart and mind. Practice making a gesture of kindness every day. In doing so, you will avoid the regrets that come from wishing you had done more for those around you, and you will experience the joy that comes from acts of kindness.

Not envious

Authentic biblical love does not envy. Pause and think for a moment. Is there anyone in your life you envy? Envy is a strong emotion of ill will pointed at someone you inwardly feel is in a higher place than you are. It is a despicable trait of being *glad* when someone experiences misfortune or pain. It is often rooted and grounded in being displeased at another's good or success. It is an embittered mind that wishes to depress the one envied to your own level instead of being willing to rise up to the level of the envied person. This is one of Satan's greatest traps to keep you down.

I vividly remember when my husband and I bought our first home. A good friend heard our good news and said, "Well, I guess I'll be the last one of us to ever get a [expletive] house." I was shocked and disturbed. She was not the kind of person who would typically use improper language. Clearly she was envious, and out of her own mouth the condition of her heart had been exposed.

Once envy is acknowledged, what do you do to get rid of these feelings of envy? Decide to delight in the esteem and honor given to someone else. Live by this decision. Trust me, your days will be much brighter. When you delight in the successes of others, it becomes fuel for your own successes. Keep a close watch on envy; this unproductive, destructive, sinful action will destroy your joy and rip at your heart. It will poison your thoughts, separate you from your friends, and fuel a lifetime of regrets. Your mind will start to fill up with thoughts of those regrets: "If only I had gone to college. If only I had married a more successful man. If only I didn't have so many bills. If only I had a better job..."

These thoughts will destroy you if you let them. Envy, when allowed to go unchecked, will fill you with all kinds of regrets that will take root in your spirit and control you. It will push people out of your life whom God intended to be there. When you decide to esteem others and celebrate their successes, you are deciding to grow in love, mature in love, and walk in love, and you will also be sharing in their joy while holding onto yours. It is through love that you and I will find our greatest life moments. It is through envy that you will collect a wasted life full of regrets.

Not boastful

Authentic biblical love does not boast. Those of us who use social media to any extent at all have probably failed this love test. We brag by uploading the best pictures of our vacation spots, our delightful meals, our beautiful children, our happy homes, the flowers our husband sent us, and on and on. *Forbes* recently reported that there is a link between Facebook and depression. They report on a study in the *Journal of Social and Clinical Psychology*, which found that there is a well-established psychological phenomenon called "social comparison," and it is this phenomenon that links time spent on Facebook with depressive symptoms.[3]

Amazing. Here again science is trying desperately to catch up with biblical wisdom. Boasting is birthed out of envy, and out of envy comes the poison of comparison, which is guaranteed to steal your joy, your peace, and your happiness and fill your life with needless regret.

Not proud or arrogant

Authentic biblical love is not proud and is not arrogant. Pride and arrogance go hand in hand, and they are both enemies of joy. The prideful nature of man is a weak attempt to cover up shortcomings, flaws, and failures. Pride and arrogance always have to have first place—in conversations and in relationships. Pride steals attention it does not deserve. Have you ever been in a conversation with someone and he raises his voice over yours or jumps in before you've finished your thought? That may seem like a small thing, but it's not. It is very telling. Or perhaps this individual holds onto silence during the conversation as a means of controlling it. Pride and arrogance destroy the joy of living, and when it comes right down to it, what has been gained?

Fight pride with humility. Every time you feel the need to be prideful or arrogant, fight it and respond with the direct opposite reaction, humility.

I once attended a luncheon, and the guest speaker was a decorator, wedding coordinator, and television personality. I have never wanted to leave an event so badly. It was absolutely horrendous. Every other sentence began with "I did," "I have," "I am," or "I know." The name-dropping and bragging were relentless. Had it not been for the kind women at my table, I would have left.

Pride and arrogance are ugly. They are presumptive. They are an obvious attempt to overinflate one's person, place, or position. Pride and arrogance come from a mind-set that says, "I can prove I'm more important than you are." Isn't that what Satan wants to prove? Doesn't he want the attention and adoration that belong to God? Doesn't he want to usurp true authority and raise himself up as God? Pride cannot stand where there is love. Love will always take its rightful position.

Not unbecoming

Authentic biblical love does not act unbecomingly. For the believer that means we should not do anything that is inappropriate, unsuitable, or ill-fitting to our beliefs. One day a woman called me, and she was totally distraught. She lost her job because, unfortunately for her, she was talking with another employee who was sharing her disgruntled opinions about their workplace as well as using foul language, and a customer overheard the conversation and turned them both in. The woman vehemently declared that she had done nothing wrong. However, her boss decided to let both women go because of their association. She was so humiliated. Humiliation sometimes comes with a hefty cost. We as believers can avoid such humiliation by deciding to walk in a way that honors God and honors people. This woman should have just walked away. There will be no regrets when we make those kinds of decisions. Authentic biblical love does not act unbecomingly.

Not self-seeking

Authentic biblical love does not seek its own interests, but instead it puts others first. It's not easy to be second. Our flesh wants to always be first, but when we put others before our own wants and desires, we better reflect Christ. An attitude and practice of selflessness is one of the most appealing characteristics we can display. It is also one that most closely reflects Christ. Self-seeking is the antithesis of love, and the only cure is to become God-seeking. When our focus is on ourselves, we cannot be happy, we cannot be fulfilled, and we cannot be productive. It takes too much energy to constantly strive for your own interests because you cannot obtain the very things you seek. Self-seeking will also cause you to focus on your regrets and try to overcome them in ineffective ways. God promises that if you will seek first the kingdom of God and His righteousness, all these things will be added to you (Matt. 6:33). In other words, God will meet your every need.

Provokes no one

Authentic biblical love does not provoke. Provocation is the act of stirring up unwanted negative emotions in others. There are some people, and I am sure you've encountered them, who love to stir the pot. They sit and wait for the opportunity to ruffle someone's feathers, so to speak. Do you know anyone like that? Are you perhaps that person? If so, you are not walking in love.

Sarah, a young woman I know, cannot go home to visit extended family at Christmas because she has a sister who loves to jab. Her sister seems delightful at first, only to then show her true colors and start attacking. She does so in the most sly and deceptive way. I know of another woman who cannot have a relationship with her mother for the very same reason. Her mother deliberately provokes her. Every visit leaves the woman feeling hurt and angry.

The Bible tells us to do all that we can do to be at peace with one another (Rom. 12:18). It does not give us license to purposely provoke another to anger. I ask you, have you ever had this happen to you? Have you ever been the one jabbing? If so, you need to stop. You are destroying yourself by allowing your thoughts and actions to be controlled by the disdain you feel for another. Heed this advice and determine to walk in love, no matter what is coming at you. Many disappointments you've felt in the past because of others will start to diminish. If you begin to respond in love, your love will grow, and as your love grows, so grows your joy, your peace, and your contentment in life.

Holds no wrongs

Authentic biblical love does not take into account a wrong suffered. This one is hard. We tend to hold people accountable for the wrongs they have committed against us. And we don't have that right. We have to let it go and grow in the love of the Lord. Unforgiveness breaks fellowship with the Lord. Unforgiveness is in direct disobedience to God. It is an act that inwardly proclaims that you are judge—but you are not. There is only one judge: the God of Abraham, Isaac, and Jacob.

Is there someone you need to forgive? If so, be quick to do it. Holding grudges will amplify your regrets. You will look back and see the missed opportunities. You will see all the treasured moments you could have enjoyed. You will see the missed blessings from a relationship that could have been restored. It will hinder your move forward. It will separate you from sweet fellowship with the Lord, and it will harden your heart.

I remember writing letters to several people who had hurt me. I never sent the letters. Later I found the letters in the closet, took them out, and read them, only to find that they were still applicable a few years later. When you have a health crisis, it's very easy to forgive—at least it was for me. Those people did not change, but I did. What once seemed so important and hurtful became so minuscule in my mind. What had once plagued me became a fading memory. Let go of all those grudges. Forgiveness is a beautiful gift from the Lord, and we must learn to exercise it.

Rejoices in truth

Authentic biblical love does not rejoice in unrighteousness but rejoices in the truth. Do you laugh at inappropriate jokes? Do you watch movies that are filled with vile behavior? Do you cheer on the actions of others that stand in direct opposition to the Word of God, or join in their celebrations? Beware. Years ago I decided that I would be cautious of what I allowed in my home. If it is not God-honoring, then it does not need to be in your house. Such decisions, either way, will affect your life and your future. God will not be mocked (Gal. 6:7). Too many times we stand on the sidelines and allow the world to tell us what is right and what is wrong. We can't live that way. We need to hate what God hates and love what God loves. In doing so, we will be rejoicing in the truth. Not only that, but once we have set this in our own minds, we will no longer waver between two opinions.

I was in a group of Christian women, and one lady said to another, "Can you believe it? Macy's son won't even let his own children go to church. Isn't that funny?" She chuckled in wicked delight. Macy was so broken that her grandchildren were not in church. She looked over at the woman who had mocked a heartbreaking situation in her life with great sadness in her eyes. You could almost see and feel the gaping wound. What kind of heart revels in and mocks the disappointments of others? Who revels in unrighteousness? Those with weak, sad, empty hearts do.

Shareworthy

Our love to God is measured by our everyday fellowship with others and the love it displays.

—Andrew Murray [4]

Bears all things

Authentic biblical love bears all things. What does it mean to bear all things? True biblical love means that you and I are to bear the burdens of others, which fulfills the *law of love* and the *law of Christ*. How important is this? It's everything. We are to share in each other's burdens. We do this every time we pray for another, every time we take dinner to someone who is sick, every time we volunteer to watch someone's children so she can catch up on rest, and every time we offer to help another.

Pillar of Abundant Living

If I give all my goods to feed the poor, and if I give my body to be burned, and have not love, it profits me nothing.

—1 Corinthians 13:3

Believes all things

Authentic biblical love believes all things. To love, you first must believe God—you believe His Word; you believe in His grace, His mercy, and His compassion. You then believe the best of others. My best friend sometimes teases me because I tend to take this one to extremes. She laughs at the Pollyanna attitude I have at times. In jest I respond back, "To the pure all things are pure." In all actuality, we are to think the best of people until given a reason to think otherwise. We are never to assume evil without cause. Living a life that is regret-free is living a life free of presumption. We should cleanse our minds of the things that taint our opinions of others and decide to assume the best of all people. In doing so, your days will be brighter. You will not be so easily offended. You will not think people are trying to hurt you. You will enjoy your days and not fall into the trap of getting mad over little things. You won't take things so personally. Believe me, in the big picture those little things really do not matter at all, so why let them ruin your day? Believe the best of others, and in this you will be displaying the very best in you.

Hopes all things

Authentic biblical love hopes all things. Walking in this kind of biblical love doesn't simply wish, but it expects all things. You can expect that your prayers are being heard. You can expect that God will move on your behalf. Expect that His promises are true and that God is working for your best interest. Biblical hope is not wishful thinking. No, it means having the expectancy in your heart that is sure because it is based on a solid foundation. It is based on the knowledge and belief that God works all things together for those who are called according to His purposes (Rom. 8:28). Therefore biblical love hopes the best because God has promised it even in the storms, trials, and disappointments of life.

Endures all things

Authentic biblical love endures all things. Turn the other cheek. Walk the extra mile. Give your cloak. Endure suffering. Endure hardship. Endure persecution. Endure. We are to endure for the sake of the gospel. We are to endure for the sake of others and for the strengthening of our own faith. We are to endure through persecution while standing firm on our beliefs. We are to endure rejection and opposition to our message. We as believers are to run our race with endurance (Heb. 12:1). How's your endurance? Have you ever felt like giving up because things have been too difficult? Don't. There is great victory on the other side of your trials.

Never Fails

Take the love test. Simply follow the list of characteristics of authentic biblical love and rate yourself on a scale of one to ten. Each day think about how well you've done and where you need to make improvements. (See the appendix for a sample daily template.) As you begin to take note, you will be astounded at how quickly you grow in your love walk. Are you fulfilling the law of Christ? Are you walking in authentic biblical love, or are your ratings on the low end of the spectrum? As you go through your days, use this as a means of evaluating your own heart. We will always find things that we need to improve upon.

This exercise is a constant reminder for me that as I walk in biblical love as laid out in Scripture, I will experience the kind of life that brings hope, peace, and joy. Living a life of biblical love means living a life that acts on behalf of others, loving with the compassion of Christ and fulfilling the law of love. In that there is no room for regret. Change the areas of weakness where you are not acting in love first by a decision of your will and second through prayer, and trust that God will sanctify you in those areas. You can live this love walk. Your life will radically change as you accept the challenge. Embrace every moment God has given you. Life is precious. This is truly what my father meant when he said on his deathbed, "I have no regrets."

INTENTIONAL LIVING

- Take the love test and rate yourself on a scale of one to ten.
- Identify your areas of weakness.
- Commit to change in those areas of weakness through prayer, Bible study, and the power of the Holy Spirit.
- Determine to let go of envy, arrogance, and pride, and not to be self-seeking or act in an unbecoming manner.
- Determine to rejoice in truth regardless of cultural mores.
- Determine to live a life of great expectation.
- Determine to bear all things and endure all things with the love and compassion of Christ.

CHAPTER 6

CHARACTER COUNTS

As the excellence of steel is strength, and
the excellence of art is beauty, so the excellence of mankind is moral character.

—A. W. TOZER[1]

FREEDOM *TODAY* WAS like my child, given as a gift from the
Lord. It was a nationally and internationally syndicated television show that aired for a number of years. I was the host
and executive producer of the show, and I would bring on guests who
shared their stories of radical, life-altering experiences. They would
share their personal testimonies of how God had brought them from
a very dark place into the light of His love. I received a call one day
from a woman named Megan who lived in Fort Worth, Texas. She
was broken. I could hardly understand her through the tears. She
had grown up in church, but through her time as a young mother
and her experience with a very bad marriage, she had walked away
from the church and the Lord. Megan had three girls and had been
through a rather brutal divorce. She was left raising her children on
her own. She worked for a very profitable company. She found out
her boss had been skimming off the business for some time. At first
Megan thought about turning him in but feared that would mean
the end of her job. After some time she decided to take a portion of
the profit for herself. For a number of years they were successful at
defrauding the company of millions. Eventually the FBI caught on
to their scheme, and they were both arrested for a host of offenses.
Megan was going to go to prison. Through her tears she cried out,
"If only...if only I would have lived my life as I knew I should have.
If only I would have made better decisions. If only I had not been so
greedy. If only I would have remained in church. If only..."

Outside of salvation, nothing will empower you to live a life without regrets more than having godly character. Character counts. Character building is an important aspect of living a life that is honorable and pleases God. God desires us to grow in character; therefore we should be constantly growing and not become stagnant in our faith. Every Christian parent desires to build in their child's heart the qualities that most reflect Christ. These characteristics will help them form and shape a future that is valuable, impactful, and purposeful. The desire should be the same for ourselves as well.

To begin to develop good character, you must understand what it is. Character is what defines you. It is the mental, moral, and ethical qualities distinctive to a particular individual. It's a person's personality, nature, and disposition. It is moral integrity. In many respects character is the outward reflection of inward righteousness. It is what people will remember about you when you are long gone. Character is important, especially if you want to live a life of no regrets. Most of us will not find our life in as much disarray as Megan, but most of us do have a bucket full of regrets. How can you live a life in such a way that you are protected from those devastating decisions? When your time here on earth is done, will you look back and feel the magnitude of a life filled with regret? We get one chance to live this life, and we want to do it in the best way possible.

A Life Without Character

Character building is important in living a life that is honorable, pleases God, and minimizes regrets. To begin to understand the importance of character, let's look at King Saul of Israel. From outward appearances Saul had it all. Chosen as the people's king, he brought Israel under a new monarchy. No longer would they be governed by judges raised up by God, but instead they would be under the leadership of a newly appointed king, chosen by man. He was tall, and according to Scripture there was not a man among the sons of Israel more handsome than he (1 Sam. 9:2). He allowed the evil of his heart, his struggle with jealousy, and his fearful nature to overtake him and destroy his legacy. He was thirty years old when he became king, and he reigned over Israel for forty-two years (1 Sam. 13:1).

Saul successfully led Israel in victory over their enemies: the Ammonites, the Philistines, the Moabites, and the Amalekites. As the women danced, they sang: "Saul has slain his thousands, and David his ten thousands" (1 Sam. 18:7). However, God would eventually reject Saul as Israel's king (1 Sam. 15:26). God reminded Samuel, the prophet who anointed Saul as king, not to look on the outside; He reminded him that God looks at the heart.

Saul was victorious, but David was even more victorious. Saul heard the celebratory cheers of victory for David after each successful battle. He felt the admiration on the rise for David in the hearts of his people. He saw their faces as they danced in the streets, and jealousy began to take root; it grew and grew and grew. Saul would be his own greatest enemy. His paramount weaknesses were jealousy, fear, and seeking wisdom apart from God. He acted in disobedience to the prophet's directive and foolishly provided for himself an unauthorized offering out of concern for the unease of the people and fear of the upcoming battle. As David, his former servant who became a mighty warrior for Israel, grew in popularity, so did the jealousy of Saul's heart. Jealousy was the beginning of his end.

Jealousy is a destiny killer. It causes regret to flourish in the heart. It will stop you before you get started, or it will bring you to an abrupt end if you have already gotten started. Jealousy will kill your joy, your peace, and your relationships. Have you ever struggled with jealousy? Have you ever been fearful that someone else might get more notoriety than you, or that they might become more well-liked than you? Envy and jealousy are demonically empowered; that is incredibly clear in Saul's life. Saul had become callous in his sin. He had become increasingly disobedient to God. His sins had become his lifestyle, his nature, a part of who he was. This downward spiral is a prime example of how sin, when it is birthed and fully grown, produces death.

Saul made a poor decision to have a medium conjure up Samuel (1 Sam. 28:11). This seeking of wisdom apart from God would be a fatal decision. The very next day that one decision cost him his life and the lives of his three sons, his armor bearer, and the men who fought with him in battle. If you are not familiar with the story, you can read the accounts in 1 Samuel chapters 8–31. If ever there is a lesson to be learned from the failure and weaknesses of Saul, it is the dire urgency and importance of growing in godly character. Our destinies may be at stake.

THE PROCESS

The Word of God lays out the clear path for character development, and it includes suffering, endurance, and hope:

> We also boast in tribulation, knowing that tribulation produces patience, patience produces character, and character produces hope. And hope does not disappoint, because the love of God is shed abroad in our hearts by the Holy Spirit who has been given to us.
> —ROMANS 5:3–5

Character building starts practically the moment we are born into this world. Babies who receive love from both parents are often more well-rounded, content, and successful as adults. They are more likely to be confident and assertive. Conversely, children who are born into a dysfunctional family, devoid of love and guidance, are more likely to struggle to find themselves or understand the direction they should go in life. The love of parents, or a single parent, is a critical aspect in character development.

Character development begins with making godly choices in every situation. I remember an incident that took place when we lived in Virginia and my son was just four years old. Logan wandered into the bathroom. I noticed he had been quiet, and after a few minutes I became concerned. I went into the bathroom and immediately noticed that the sink was almost filled to overflowing.

"Logan, what are you doing, son?"

"Mommy, I am mixing chemicals."

"Oh no!"

I went over and peered into the overflowing sink, and sure enough, it was filled with chemicals—every perfume, face cleanser, skin moisturizer, hand softener, and liquid foundation I owned had been added in.

"Logan, why are you doing this, son? There must be hundreds of dollars' worth of product poured into this sink, and now it's all totally useless."

I picked him up and carried him to the bed and told him that I was greatly disappointed because he knew he should not have done that. With all sincerity I gazed into his precious little eyes, and he said, "Mommy, you don't want to prevent me from becoming a scientist, do you?" I knew then that I was in trouble, being outwitted by a four-year-old. It was a day of character building for both of us. Logan knew better even at his young age. For me, my character was being tested. Would I bring clear correction as I knew in my heart I should do, or would I give in to that smile that melted my heart and miss the opportunity to bring discipline so that it would not happen again? Sometimes doing what is right is hard to do, but it is always the best decision. If something costs you enough, you will learn to not do it, or you will learn to do things correctly so that you will not have to keep paying the price.

We learn from the Bible and from instruction. We learn from our parents, and we learn from teachers and coaches. We learn from our mistakes. Or perhaps we choose not to learn and keep on paying for our mistakes. As long as we learn from our mistakes, we do not have to regret them because of the valuable life lessons we take away from the experience. On the other hand, heartache and regret come when we fail to learn from our mistakes and constantly repeat them over and over again.

Shareworthy

Character is not who you are in the light, but what shines through in the midst of utter darkness.

—Robin Bertram

REFLECTION

Christian pastor and prolific author A. W. Tozer once said, "A pharisee is hard on others and easy on himself, but a spiritual man is easy on others and hard on himself."[2] This hints at the truth that one of the most important aspects of character building is admitting mistakes. You cannot change what you are unwilling to acknowledge. Most of our mistakes stem from our attempts to fill the void from something that is missing inside of us. We attempt to fill the void with inappropriate relationships, alcohol, drugs, cigarettes, excessive shopping, excessive golfing, overeating, overworking, or overdoing anything, although that hole cannot be filled by anything other than God. We tend to blame others for our issues, but when we take a long hard look, we see the part we play as well. Character building will begin in us as we acknowledge and take responsibility for our own mistakes without blame.

If you look back at the mistakes that you have made, have you learned from them, or are you still making the same mistakes? True reflection will help you to be honest with yourself, and it will help you put things into perspective. You may have heard the expression that your heart is your best compass. That's a lie; our hearts are deceitfully wicked. The Word of God is the best compass.

Suffering

Your character is defined by the way you go through and come out of the adversities of life. Character matters. The Word teaches us that we will suffer, but in that suffering we will learn and grow in endurance.

I don't want to suffer. My prayer has often been, "Lord, teach me, but from Your Word rather than from Your discipline, and teach me in Your great mercy." Suffering sometimes happens because of something we ourselves cause, but sometimes it is outside of our control. Either way, God confirms in His Word that suffering is a part of our human existence, and we can learn and grow in the midst of it. Nobody likes to suffer, but suffering will produce a good result in you. We all understand suffering that results from bad decisions because we know we reap what we sow. We understand suffering when it comes from discipline. We understand that persecution causes suffering as we stand for righteousness's sake, as all who desire to live a godly life in Jesus will most assuredly be persecuted (2 Tim.

3:12). But what about suffering when you've done no wrong? First Peter 2:20 confirms that if you suffer for doing good, it is commendable before God. Have you ever really suffered for doing good?

My friend Katie was an instructor at a health and wellness gym. She would often play contemporary Christian music as she taught the class. One morning there was a large sign that said, "Any music that contains the name of Jesus or any curse words is forbidden to be used for workouts." Katie went promptly to the director of the facility and questioned why there had been a change in the policy. Up until that point the instructors could choose any music they liked, and their attendees had the liberty of choosing which instructor they preferred. Her director explained that there had been a complaint, and that single voice prompted the new policy. This was infringement on personal liberties taken too far. The freedom to decide was now limited by one person's opinion. Did Katie suffer? You bet she did. She immediately turned in her notice. I wish I could say that she got a new job, one that was better, but she didn't. However, that decision was one that she never regretted. Sometimes doing the right thing will cost us greatly, but the rewards will always outweigh the losses in the long run.

Shareworthy

Character cannot be developed in ease and quiet. Only through experience of trial and suffering can the soul be strengthened, ambition inspired, and success achieved.

—Helen Keller[3]

ENDURANCE

There is good news. Suffering produces endurance. I've never been much of an athlete, but I know that when I exercise, I cannot start off running a 10K. I have to work up to it. If I tried to run a 10K on day one, I'd be out almost before I even began. Preparation is necessary for endurance. Marathoners devote much of their time to running many miles in preparation for a long run; however, it does not stop there. They also may train by performing challenging threshold runs where they really push themselves for speed and agility during the last portion of their practice runs. When they are physically and mentally worn down, that would be considered a good practice, which would in turn give them a leg up on race day. Endurance is everything. The same is true for us in life. We have to adequately prepare for the race that lies before us so that we can finish well.

Pillar of Abundant Living

Do you not know that all those who run in a race run, but one receives the prize? So run, that you may obtain it. Everyone who strives for the prize exercises self-control in all things. Now they do it to obtain a corruptible crown, but we an incorruptible one. So, therefore, I run, not with uncertainty. So I fight, not as one who beats the air. But I bring and keep my body under subjection, lest when preaching to others I myself should be disqualified.

—1 Corinthians 9:24–27

We are to train but not aimlessly. We are to train with focus and discipline so that we grow in endurance. We are to press forward, forgetting the things that lie behind us: our hurts, our failures, and our disappointments. We are to strain forward to what lies ahead, which is the goal of the prize of God's heavenly calling in Jesus. It's hard to press forward when we are focused on what is behind. A good runner doesn't visualize where competitors are behind him. No, he keeps his eyes on the finish line and the prize to come at the end of that run.

Regrets take a looking-backward approach to life rather than a looking-forward approach. If you are constantly looking backward, you cannot adequately move forward. Your stride will be hindered. You will lose focus and have little endurance. You will have your eyes on man instead of the prize that awaits you. If you want to live a life that pleases God, is focused on Jesus Christ, and is not filled with regret, then forget what is behind. Look to what is ahead and run the race in order to receive the prize that awaits you. Your character is defined and refined by your endurance while walking through the challenges of godly discipline and suffering. Walk wisely. How you respond will define who you are becoming. How you respond today will determine the outcome of tomorrow. Run your race. It's the only one that will count in eternity.

CHARACTER

Endurance builds character in you. Character is not about how you appear to others; it's how you act when nobody is watching. Character is not who you are in the light, but what shines through in the midst of utter darkness. Character is hidden deep, is revealed in the worst of times, and reflects the heart of a man. Character is the aggregate of the way you choose to treat people, how you maneuver through the storms of life, and the way you behave under pressure.

If we look again at the life of Saul, we see that he was so afraid of David that he plotted to kill him, using his own daughter as bait. Saul offered David his daughter if he could slay one hundred Philistines in hopes David would be killed by the Philistines instead (1 Sam. 18). Saul was not interested in being victorious over his real enemy, but instead he was interested in seeing his best warrior die at the hand of the enemy. Our fears will cause us to focus on the wrong enemy, and our fears and jealousies will cause us to act against our own best interests. Saul was weak, fearful, and jealous. He had lost fellowship with the Lord. Could it be that this mighty king, handsome in appearance, the people's king, was now no more than a murderous thug? His plan backfired. God was with David. Saul's daughter, Michal, loved David, and David became even more successful. His fame continued to grow. Saul, on the other hand, became even more fearful than before, making one bad decision after another. Character matters.

Shareworthy

A good character is the best tombstone. Those who loved you and were helped by you will remember you when forget-me-nots have withered. Carve your name on hearts, not on marble.

—Charles Spurgeon[4]

Authentic Christian character is based on our commitment to Christ. It begins with salvation and encompasses the process of sanctification as we walk with the Lord. We go through a cleansing process the moment we are born again, and then we grow in Christlikeness as we grow in understanding and devotion to Him. You will either be moving toward Christ or away from Him; there is no standing still. Your reputation is what others think of you, but it often has very little to do with who you really are. Godly character is what you are when you've been tried and proven. It is not what you say you are or what people think you are; instead, it is what shines through after you have suffered and have endured. It is the proof of your genuineness.

Pillar of Abundant Living

For this very reason make every effort to add virtue to your faith; and to your virtue, knowledge; and to your knowledge, self-control; and to your self-control, patient endurance; and to your patient endurance, godliness; and to your godliness, brotherly kindness; and to your brotherly kindness, love.

—2 Peter 1:5–7

Shareworthy

The believer's hope is not a frail, weak hope. No, it is the assurance of a secure future, a perennial hope, as well as a hope in our living Savior for abundant life in the here and now.

—Robin Bertram

HOPE

Character produces hope. Hope is the benefit and outcome of godly character development. Every day during the trial concerning my health, when I came home, I saw a sign on the property of a home being built in my neighborhood. The sign was rather large and stationed on the corner of the property. You could not miss it. It read in large print, "ALS." While those were simply the initials of the builder who was building the home, it was also a reminder of the mountain that stood in my way. I wanted desperately to tear it down. As I struggled for over a year, I had to pass by that sign on a daily basis. There was no other way to get home. One day shortly after I was seeing greater weakness coming on, I remember crying out to God, "God, I have no hope. I cannot see. Please give me eyes to see. Please give me hope again."

Living without hope is like being shut and buried in a coffin, but you are still alive, stuck inside. That's how I felt. Those were some of the darkest days of my life. I felt as if I could not breathe, as if I could not see. Worst of all, I could not hope. "God, where are you?" I asked.

Hope was nowhere to be found, although I knew in my heart that God was with me. Hear me: life without hope is a terrible way to live. While the hope of eternal life was settled in my heart, I was looking at the real possibility of life here ending. What an eye opener. We think we will never see that day, but we all certainly will. After I prayed for hope, God began to give me glimmers of hope.

I noticed one day that the ALS sign had been removed, although there was still some work left on the house. Something rose up in me and I wanted to shout, "Hallelujah!" My physical issues were still present, but something in my heart was allowing me to see again. My hope was returning. When the sign came down, I declared by faith that I was healed, that the terrible nightmare was over, and that I was going to live. The sign coming down was more than a spiritual sign or implication; it was an answered prayer. I grabbed onto it and declared my healing. I still had struggles ahead, and I knew that, but at least I could see. Did my healing come immediately? No, but I did believe that it would come, and thank God it did.

Your character is defined by the hope that you embrace while there seems to be no hope at all. The believer's hope is not a frail, weak hope. No, it is the assurance of a secure future, a perennial hope, as well as a hope in our living Savior for abundant life in the here and now. During my struggle with illness God was with me. God walked me through the valley of the shadow of death, just as David penned in the Psalms, and God alone was my rod and my staff, leading and guiding me (Ps. 23:4). In the fires of refinement or the fires of affliction God will be with you, and how you choose to respond may very well determine your outcome.

Through my experience I determined in my heart that not one day would go by without my being verbally thankful to God for life, for breath, and for all the tremendous blessings He has given me. I made a decision to live and to live well for the Lord. I decided to celebrate everything of beauty in creation that He has placed around me: the wispy Spanish moss that hangs from the trees, the horses that gallop in the field behind my home, and the sound of the birds as they sing first thing in the morning. I will treasure the gifts that God has graciously given and refuse to go through my day as though those miracles of God are unimportant. He has put those things on this earth for you and me to enjoy. You do not realize how important the small things in life are until they are taken from you. I learned through this experience to never give up on hope. I learned that as long as there is breath in my body, hope is available. Hope is not wishful thinking but a confident expectation that God will move on my behalf. He will move on your behalf too. Take sound advice and enjoy today; embrace and celebrate the small things in life, and hold on to your eternal hope in Jesus Christ regardless of your circumstances because He is working on your behalf.

REGRETS DISAPPOINT

"The LORD would have established your kingdom over Israel forever. But now your kingdom will not continue" (1 Sam. 13:13–14). These harsh words were for Saul. He and his entire family lost out because of lack of character. His life came to an abrupt end and his legacy was marred into eternity. David, who eventually took Saul's place as king of Israel, had his own weaknesses: an affair with Bathsheba led to him killing her husband by putting him on the front lines of battle and caused the death of David's firstborn child—all because of his sins (2 Sam. 11–12). However, David did not allow his weaknesses to define him. What was the difference? David, although it took him some time, repented of the evil he had committed. He was truly remorseful and sought God for forgiveness. David knew how God treated sin. He knew that when sin was confessed and the heart turned away from that sin, God would remove it as far as the east is from the west. He knew that God would remember his sin no more. David knew that the way to cleanse his life from regret was to truly submit his shortcomings, his weaknesses, and his sin to God and allow the disciplinary hand of God to remold his future. Saul, on the other hand, carried his weaknesses, his shortcomings, and his sin to his grave, leaving a legacy of failure in his wake.

Your character is defined by how you choose to allow life to define you. You can choose to become bitter or better, defeated or victorious, wrapped up in bondage or free. You can choose to sit in remorse and allow your mistakes to define you, or you can learn from your failures and turn them into opportunities to grow and help others grow. You can wallow in regrets of the past, or you can rise above the drama and trauma and embrace life. These choices will determine if you are immobilized by loss or propelled by opportunity. Put the past in the past. Move into your future with vigor, and allow the lessons that you have learned to be cobblestones on your path to a bright and productive future for the Lord. Live with no more regrets, only life lessons with godly purposes blossoming forth.

We learn from Saul that life is not always about how well you start, but rather how well you finish, and the way you finish will be determined by the decisions you make today. Choose to make decisions that will be honoring to God. Choose to make decisions based on the written Word of God. Choose to make decisions that are led by the direction of the Holy Spirit. I do not want to hear one day, "Away from Me, I never knew you" (Matt. 7:23, author's paraphrase). Rather, I want to stand before Jesus one day and hear, "Well done, good and faithful servant" (Matt. 25:23). Now that's a life well lived. "Character in a saint means the disposition of Jesus Christ persistently manifested."[5]

Intentional Living

- Character is built, not acquired; therefore make decisions based on godly principles found in Scripture.
- Character comes through the pain of suffering, so do not run from it; instead, learn the lessons along the way.
- Character comes through endurance, and you must train like an athlete; determine to practice righteousness daily.
- Character comes as you choose to follow the mandates of Scripture, so choose to be obedient in every area of your life.
- Character comes as you look ahead, press forward, and refuse to look back, so keep your eyes looking toward a hopeful future regardless of your circumstances.
- Character comes as you refuse to allow your life's circumstances to define you; instead, allow God's promises found in Scripture to refine and define your future, which is good.
- Character is not about how you start; it's about how you finish, so determine to finish well by living each and every day with a thankful heart.

CHAPTER 7

ABUNDANT JOY

Joy is prayer—Joy is strength—Joy is love—Joy is a net of love by which you can catch souls. God loves a cheerful giver. She gives most who gives with joy. The best way to show our gratitude to God and the people is to accept everything with joy. A joyful heart is the inevitable result of a heart burning with love. Never let anything so fill you with sorrow as to make you forget the joy of the Christ risen.

—MOTHER TERESA[1]

WHEN I DIE, I want to know that I have truly lived. One of the worst things that can happen is to wake up one day and realize you have not enjoyed life. We often go through life with our checklists, thinking about the next thing on our agenda or the work we have to finish throughout our day. We frequently forget to enjoy the small things in life. While that description characterized me at times, I can finally say that my heart is full. The struggles I have had certainly pale in comparison to the joy I have in my intimate knowledge of my heavenly Father, my Lord, my Savior. Through that intimacy God has taught me how to embrace everyday life with joy, regardless of my circumstances.

A PERFECT DAY

What is joy? How do you walk in it? Can you really stop being anxious and enjoy life regardless of circumstances? These are just a few questions I asked myself as I was facing the mountain of health problems that stood before me. I began to think about my days. How would you describe the perfect day?

When I think of a perfect day, I remember when my children were small and we lived in southeast Georgia on a marsh. Our backyard overlooked a golf course in St. Marys, Georgia. Our home had a large, two-story window in the family room, and as you looked out, you could see across the marsh into Florida. You may know that Florida is the lightning capital of the United States. Floridians experience lightning almost one-third of the days in a given year.[2] The Atlantic Ocean on the east and the Gulf Coast to the west help to keep the environment warm and moist, creating conditions conducive to thunderstorms. As a family we would gather in the family room and watch those thunderstorms. It never got old for us. We did it every time there was a storm. And then around dinnertime every night a family of raccoons would make their way across the fairway through our backyard and over to our neighbor's house where they would find food that had been left out for them. They were arranged like stair steps—dad, mom, big brother, and three smaller raccoons—all hunched over, waddling in a row down the same path night after night for dinner. My children, either Taylor or Logan, would announce their appearance, and we would all run to the window and watch them. This too never grew old, and every night we would gather at the window and watch: another perfect day.

What would a joy-filled day look like to you? Do you think you would have a greater sense of joy if you could see the world? I have been blessed to travel around the world. I have parasailed in Hawaii, zip-lined in Costa Rica, and hiked through the rain forest. I have taken a gondola through the Grand Canal of Venice and have been blessed by the pope. I have carried a wooden cross through the streets of London. I have survived in the jungles of Africa and had Bible study in a bomb shelter in a kibbutz in Israel. I have experienced things that many people only dream about, but I can tell you with all confidence that it is not money, travel, or fame that gives joy. It is the small things in life, if we choose to the take the time to notice them, that offer the greatest joy. It is the love of a family member, the smile on a baby's face, or the hug of an old acquaintance. It is a telephone call from a friend when you are feeling lonely. Again, it is the small things in life that will bring the greatest joy. So I ask you, are you enjoying life, or are you waiting for your life to just get better?

Joy Unspeakable

Have you truly experienced joy? Do you know what joy is and what it isn't? Do you want to cultivate a lifestyle of joy that will allow you to avoid those "if only" regrets? Let's look at how to experience true joy even in the midst of pain, struggle, and challenges. Together let's identify some potential joy thieves, and then I will share seven keys to being restored in the fullness of joy, no longer wavering but being empowered to abide and rest in a constant state of joy. We begin to experience true joy when we rest in God. As Scripture says, "For I satiate the weary souls and I replenish every languishing soul" (Jer. 31:25). It is in the absence of worry, guilt, and shame that we begin to build a foundation and basis for a joy-filled existence.

Joy is a fruit of the Holy Spirit, which is most greatly experienced by those willing to surrender all self-sufficiency, self-promotion, self-reliance, self-protection, and self-absorption. It is a gift. Being joyful is to be glad or to rejoice, with the connotation that implies to dance for joy or to spin around with pleasure. Can't you just visualize little children playing together on a playground, participating in the purest form of joy, laughter, and glee: little girls holding hands and spinning as fast as they can in a circle? I want you to imagine a day like that in your own life, perhaps when you were just a little child. Think back. Can you remember a day like that?

When my children were small, we would go to Disney World, and Logan and Taylor would love to find waterspouts that were synchronized to music and jump on them before they were about to blow. I remember loving to watch them giggle over something so simple. With all the rides, the attractions, and the shows it was that time playing in the waterspouts that was one of the highlights of our yearly visit to the park. I firmly believe this is how we are to live our lives. I believe we are to live each and every day as if it were our last, embracing the small things life has to offer. How would your life be different? Would your days be filled with worry, anxiety, or fear, or would they be filled with peace and love and laughter?

Pillar of Abundant Living

Rejoice in the Lord always. Again I will say, rejoice! Let everyone come to know your gentleness. The Lord is at hand. Be anxious for nothing, but in everything, by prayer and supplication with gratitude, make your requests known to God. And the peace of God, which surpasses all understanding, will protect your hearts and minds through Christ Jesus.

—Philippians 4:4–7

Rejoice; the Lord is near. Joy is an emotion that inspires our most unselfish desires and motivates us to live well and give to others what we have been given. It subdues the anxious heart. Joy is an abiding sense of well-being that is more than happiness; it is deep and rich and results in the confident security of a good future. Joy is the outcome and fruit of the indwelling Holy Spirit. Joy is contagious. As defined in the *New Unger's Bible Dictionary, joy* is "a delight of the mind arising from the consideration of a present or assured possession of a good future."[3] However, I have my own definition: Joy is a stable, underlying emotion or condition of well-being that is rooted and grounded in an outlook on life from a heavenly perspective. It cannot be shaken.

Finding Joy

The Lord intended for us to live in the joy of His Spirit and the joy of our salvation. Enjoy this moment. Enjoy this day—it's one you will never get back. As Ecclesiastes says, "There is nothing better than to be happy and enjoy ourselves as long as we can" (Eccles. 3:12, NLT). Here are seven keys to experiencing life's greatest joys.

Key #1: Start with salvation

Once a person is born again, his eyes are opened to how much he is loved and his own worth. His eyes are opened to a secure future no matter the circumstances. He learns of the promise of heaven and can overcome the fear of death. Being born again allows your heart to receive and to give love. You may have a sense of being loved by your parents, or family and friends, but to be born again and understand the deep, abiding love that God has for His children takes love to a whole new level. It's a love that is unconditional. It is a pure love that cannot be taken away.

Happiness is not the same as joy. Happiness is a volatile emotion that can be driven away by circumstances. To some degree it is reliant on those around you as well as your current position in life. Difficult relationships or family members who cause strife weigh on your emotions and can significantly affect your happiness. There are some circumstances you can change, and there are some circumstances you cannot change; regardless, the challenge is to refuse to allow circumstances to steal your joy. Circumstances can steal your happiness but not your joy unless you allow it. Joy is not trapped by the confines of your present situation; it is deeply rooted and grounded in the confidence you have in Jesus Christ through the power of the Holy Spirit.

Key #2: Walk in joy

It is your choice to walk in joy or not. How do you choose joy? First of all, acknowledge in your heart that the Lord is near you. He sticks closer to you than a brother. He has promised to never leave or forsake you (Deut. 31:6). He has promised to walk with you and be a light on the path that you have to walk. Does that bring a sense of peace and well-being? Can you feel His presence? His presence in your life will bring about great joy.

Several years ago I was praying one morning during a time of worship, and I told God that when I got to heaven, I wanted to dance for joy unto Him. I lifted my head and looked up to the sky and saw the clouds had formed what looked like a stairway to heaven. I had never seen anything like it before nor have I seen anything like it since. I had a vision of a ballerina elegantly dancing up the staircase of clouds into the heavens, and then I bowed my head and wept. It was the most beautiful thing I had ever seen, and I knew God had answered my prayer. I was so humbled and overwhelmed by His goodness.

This taught me in a greater way how intricately God is involved in our lives. He directed my prayer that day. He formed the clouds, and He gave me an open vision of a beautiful ballerina dancing toward heaven. I believe God speaks to us in different ways. I am a visual person, so He gave me a vision that I could relate to. My joy was being made complete as I understood just how much He loved me. He loves you too. He wants you to feel that kind of deep, abiding joy that comes from being in His presence.

Pillar of Abundant Living

You will make known to me the path of life; in Your presence is fullness of joy; at Your right hand there are pleasures for evermore.

—Psalm 16:11

Key #3: Choose to be in His presence

Abiding joy comes from being in His presence; choose to do this on a daily basis. Develop a systematic time and place to enter into His presence. King David tells us in the Psalms that he would come early in the morning (Ps. 63:1). Do you have a time and place to meet with God daily? If not, there is no time like the present. Some of my most joyful experiences were spent in the presence of God. When my children were young, I spent much of my time with Him in my Suburban. I would drop my children off at school and come home and sit in my vehicle for hours. I know that sounds very odd, but I would listen to praise and worship music on the way home, and before I knew it, God was in the Suburban with me. Through this I learned that God is present in the midst of praise and worship. It does not have to be just at church. It can be in your home, in your closet, or in your car. I praise God while grocery shopping. I love going to the grocery store. Some see it as a chore, but that's not the case for me. I walk down the aisles and thank and praise Him, and before you know it, I'm having church in the frozen food section. It can be wherever and whenever you want to lift Him up in praise and adoration.

Just start praising Him wherever you go. You will begin to feel His presence and love in a tangible way—no worries, no concerns, no stress, just pure love. Now that's joy.

Key #4: Do not worry

Refuse to give in to worry. To experience abiding joy, you have to determine in your heart that you will not worry. Worry kills. It can literally make you sick. It causes you to be less of a mother, less of a wife, less of a sister, less of a father, less of a brother, or less of a friend. Worry disrupts your future. It puts things on hold and causes you to be less effective, less influential, and less productive. Worry and anxiety weigh down the heart. Perhaps you have big issues going on in your life; trust me, I've been there. I have had struggles that are too deep, too personal, and too painful to share here. Through it all I have learned to trust in Jesus. Worry says to God, "You are not sufficient to meet my needs. I need a plan, God, and that plan does not involve You."

Do not worry. Give your burdens to the Lord. Be anxious for nothing (Phil. 4:6). Scripture tells us this emphatically. If you are a believer in Jesus Christ, you don't have to live with anxiety because you have His Spirit dwelling in you and with you. Make a conscious effort daily to give your burdens to Him. If you live a life of worry and anxiety, then you will most assuredly be focused on regrets. Regrets steal your joy. Decide today to enjoy every moment God gives you.

Here are some ways that you can be free from anxieties and worry:

+ Accept in your heart that this unrealistic thought process of constant worry is not of God. It stands in opposition to faith, and it refuses to acknowledge the supremacy and providence of God. God is in control, and that should give you great comfort even in the midst of a storm.
+ Confess the sin of being anxious.
+ Acknowledge the sovereignty of God in all situations.

- Reject the spirit of fear that has dominated your thought processes.
- Decide to fight the negative thoughts by actively casting them down.
- Replace those anxious thoughts with good thoughts and the truth of God's Word.

Key #5: Take everything to God in prayer

To experience true joy, you must take everything to God in prayer with thanksgiving and know that He hears you (Phil. 4:6). I pray about everything. I pray in the shower. I pray when I am out walking and when I am doing chores around my home. I've mastered the "pray without ceasing" thing because I have come to recognize how much I need it (1 Thess. 5:17). Prayer is a necessity in my life. You too need to master the command to "pray without ceasing." God is worthy to be acknowledged in everything.

Personally I struggled with giving thanks in prayer, a command given in the verse after "pray without ceasing" (1 Thess. 5:18). When I have had difficulties of great magnitude, I sometimes have forgotten to be thankful. Giving thanks is necessary because if you cannot thank God for the good He has already given you, why do you think you deserve to have Him do even more good for you? I sometimes catch myself asking for something before I thank Him for what He has already given. The danger of familiarity can sometimes cause you to fail to fear God—that is, stand in awe of Him. God is glorified when we show the reverence due Him. What I have learned from walking with God for many years is that He demands a thankful heart. It's the very least we can do.

Key #6: Identify joy stealers

I was ministering to a woman who had been struggling with depression when the Lord prompted me to ask her about her childhood and divorce. Her husband left her for another woman years before, but she still carried guilt for not being the wife and mother she thought she should have been. She struggled with abandonment issues that went back as far as her childhood because of her parents' actions. Although she said she had forgiven them, there was a hint of disdain in her voice. I prayed with her and asked her if she would be willing to forgive them and give up the blame, guilt, and regrets she had been carrying. I explained that once she had confessed her sins to God, she was actually sinning against Him by holding herself in unforgiveness when He had already forgiven her. She had exalted her opinions over His righteous judgment and placed herself as judge.

"Did God forgive you when you asked Him to?"

"Yes," she said.

"How do you know?" I asked.

"Because the Bible says that He is faithful and just to forgive us our sins when we ask."

"Then why are you holding judgment against yourself?"

She started to weep. We prayed again, this time with true forgiveness toward all involved, even herself. Then she shouted, "I am free. I feel such peace. I am free."

Shareworthy

I was delivered from the burden that had so heavily suppressed me. The spirit of mourning was taken from me, and I knew what it was to truly rejoice in God my Savior.

—George Whitfield [4]

There are joy stealers. That doesn't mean that joy is totally taken from us, but rather our joy is suppressed when we live in deception, oppression, or crisis with repeated failures and broken dreams. Our joy is suppressed when we live a life of regret without a God-given purpose. As destructive as they seem, these issues do not destroy your inner faith, but they do suppress your joy. If they are allowed to linger, they can block you to where you can no longer feel joy. Unforgiveness, bitterness, blame, regret, guilt, shame, and worldly remorse may steal your joy. Remove them. Make the decision today to repent and move on. The apostle Paul instructs believers to forget what is behind, reach forward to what lies ahead, and press toward the goal to win the prize of God's heavenly calling in Jesus Christ (Phil. 3:13–14).

Pillar of Abundant Living

Finally, brothers, whatever things are true, whatever things are honest, whatever things are just, whatever things are pure, whatever things are lovely, whatever things are of good report, if there is any virtue, and if there is any praise, think on these things.

—Philippians 4:8

Key #7: Build joy

Devise a strategy for joy building. Ask yourself what brings you the most joy. Serving God and being with my family come in first for me. There is no greater joy than sharing the good news of the gospel. Think about it—we get to participate in the greatest blessing in a person's life. What joy! Learn to share the gospel, and your joy will be increased exponentially. Start to build a life full of joy and free of regrets.

I love to read my Bible. It is a time when my spirit is renewed and energized; joy inside starts to bubble up as I read and study. I was talking recently with a woman who loves to read Christian books but rarely reads her Bible. Christian books are great, but they should not be a substitute for the Word of God because they often contain more of man and less of the cleansing Word. What happens to your physical body when you go two or three days without feeding it? Well, the same thing happens to your spirit when you do not take the time to feed it with the Word. Spending time in the Word will most assuredly bring you that inner strength and joy.

The next thing that I absolutely love is to use my God-given gifts. I am a teacher at heart, so teaching Bible classes brings me great joy. What has God put you here on the earth to do? It is extremely important to find your purpose in life. When you do find it, it will bring you great joy.

If you want to grow in the joy you've already been given through Jesus Christ, then learn to share the gospel, spend time in His Word daily, use your spiritual gifts for His glory, and find your purpose in life.

Use these seven keys to grow in the fullness of joy and learn to walk in a life filled with hope and promise. Lay down any regret you've been carrying. Put it behind you. Walk in the joy of your salvation, and determine that this is the day the Lord has made and you will be glad and rejoice in it. God intended for our days to be satisfying. He intended for us to live in the joy of His Spirit and the joy of our salvation. Enjoy this moment. Enjoy this day: it's one you can never get back.

Pillar of Abundant Living

So I concluded there is nothing better than to be happy and enjoy ourselves as long as we can. And people should eat and drink and enjoy the fruits of their labor, for these are gifts from God.

—Ecclesiastes 3:12–13, NLT

Intentional Living

- If you haven't already, come to God for salvation. Salvation is critical to experiencing true joy.
- Choose to walk in joy no matter the circumstances.
- Choose to be in His presence daily to experience your greatest joy.
- Refuse to give into worry; it's a vicious trap. Be freed of living an anxious life by acknowledging God's power to meet your needs and His sovereignty over all things.
- Take everything to God in prayer.
- Identify the joy stealers in your life.
- Devise a plan to build joy; include sharing the gospel, reading the Bible daily, using your spiritual gifts, and finding your God-given purpose in life.

CHAPTER 8

FORGIVE AND FORGET

*"I can forgive, but I cannot forget," is only another
way of saying, "I will not forgive." A forgiveness ought
to be like a cancelled note, torn in two and burned
up, so that it never can be shown against the man.*

—HENRY WARD BEECHER[1]

I WANT YOU TO go to Bethany and ask her for forgiveness." This
was the Holy Spirit's word to me early one morning when I met
with Him in prayer.

"For what, Lord?" I said. "I've done nothing to her. Why should I
have to go? I won't."

He said, "I want you to go and ask Bethany to forgive you."

I continued to reason, "But, Lord, it's not me; it's her. I don't have
anything against her."

"You will go," He said.

"Yes, Lord, I will go."

Pillar of Abundant Living

For if you forgive other people when they sin against
you, your heavenly Father will also forgive you. But if
you do not forgive others their sins, your Father will
not forgive your sins.

—Matthew 6:14–15, NIV

FORGIVEN

I called Bethany and set up a time and place, and several days later
we met for lunch. She came into the restaurant and welcomed me
with a hug and a big smile. We lived near each other, went to the

same church, and went to the same social events. Yet despite her smile, she had resentment toward me, and I really did not know why. All the while I was thinking, "Why in the world am I even here?" Do you have those kinds of relationships that make you cringe on the inside because you know the other people just do not like you? You're not sure why, but you are certain. This was one of those.

I smiled, and we exchanged pleasantries. We talked about our children, our husbands, and the weather. Then out of the blue I heard that still, small voice inside of my heart, "Ask her to forgive you."

I heeded the call: "Bethany, will you please forgive me?"

"For what?" she asked.

"I'm not really sure, but I know that I have hurt you in some way. I am very sorry."

Bethany bowed her head to the table and began to weep profusely. I sat there in utter shock. This was no small thing. After she gained her composure, she looked up at me and said, "I've been so jealous of you because you are so much more spiritual than I am."

"What? You've got to be kidding me, right?"

I remembered going to a Friday night social; I just happened to show up at the exact moment Bethany was telling everyone an inappropriate joke, one that should not be coming out of the mouth of a believer, especially one who was active in the church. She looked me in the eye that night, and I am sure she saw the disappointment on my face. She had been drinking that night also, another unacceptable practice for someone involved with ministry. But in her mind it was just a few casual beers with neighborhood friends. It dawned on me that this was the night when Satan had planted a seed of resentment in her heart toward me.

It would be just weeks after that lunch that God allowed me to pray with her. She decided never to drink again. Her heart was so remorseful for her actions.

God is faithful, and our obedience is everything. Forgiveness is freeing. Forgiveness unlocks the chains that hold you captive to another's influence. Forgiveness is the agent by which God allows healing and joy to come to your inner man. You are free, so be quick to forgive.

INFINITY

Why is forgiveness important? First of all, you and I have been forgiven. God said in His Word that He would remove our transgressions from us as far as the east is from the west. Imagine a straight line; if you remember geometry, then you know the line goes on infinitely. There is no stopping place on either side of that line. God says that He removes our transgressions as far as that line can travel into infinity. How great is His love! When we accept Jesus as Lord and Savior, our sins are gone, wiped away forever, and forgotten in the mind of God. The Bible reads that when "we confess our sins, He is faithful and just to forgive us our sins and cleanse us from all unrighteousness" (1 John 1:9). Sin is heavy and binding. It produces death, and nothing good comes from it. We know that sin is pleasurable for a season, but it always comes with a cost. The beauty of the gospel is that with a simple, heartfelt confession the penalty for that sin is wiped away. What price did God have to pay for the penalty of your sin and mine? We know that it cost Him Jesus Christ, His only begotten Son, dying on a bloody cross. Sin comes with a high cost.

LOVING LOGAN

I don't know about you, but my son is everything to me. He was the joy of my life from the time he entered this world, and even before he was born, I knew he was very special, a gift from God. *Nathaniel*, his middle name, means "a gift from God." I remember when we were still in the hospital, the nurses came to me and said they had never seen a newborn who could lift his upper body up and look around the room. He was strong and alert and hungry. Then when he was just sixteen months old, he read the word *collection* on a package in Walmart, and I thought I was going to faint. I knew my baby boy was very special.

How hard would it be to see your child hanging on a cross, bloody, beaten, bruised, spat on, and mocked? Hard. It would be very hard. My heart hurts to even think about that. If you have a son, then you know what I mean. Our minds cannot even fathom that kind of torture because it is foreign and incredibly brutal. To take on the penalty for our sins cost God a great deal. It was not an easy thing to do; He hung His own Son on that cross. Clearly the Roman soldiers crucified Jesus; so did the Jewish mob that cried out to free Barabbas, the insurgent, and so did you and I through our sinful nature. But ultimately it was God who devised the plan for fallen man before the world was even spoken into existence. It was truly the greatest of sacrifices.

Shareworthy

Beware of the pleasant view of the fatherhood of God: God is so kind and loving that of course, He will forgive us. That thought, based solely on emotion, cannot be found anywhere in the New Testament. The only basis on which God can forgive us is the tremendous tragedy of the Cross of Christ.

—Oswald Chambers [2]

If God was willing to pay the highest price for our forgiveness through the blood of His own Son, then how can we as believers in Jesus Christ hold forgiveness from another? Forgiving others as we have been forgiven is core in our Christian faith (Eph. 4:32). It is an absolute command. It is the very essence of who we are.

FORGIVE DEEPLY

Let's look for just a moment at one perfect example in Scripture, found in Genesis 37–47, of a willing heart in the midst of sheer hostility and hatred. Joseph, one of the twelve sons of the patriarch Jacob, was loved by his father more than his brothers: "Now Israel loved Joseph more than all his sons, because he was the son of his old age, and he made him a coat of many colors. But when his brothers saw that their father loved him more than all his brothers, they hated him and could not speak peaceably to him" (Gen. 37:3–4). Joseph's brothers were jealous, and they betrayed Joseph and sold him as a slave to be taken into Egypt. Joseph was stripped of his coat of many colors, of his authority, and of his favor. He was stripped of what was rightfully his. Years later Joseph rose to prominence in Egypt, and as his dream foretold, he had power over his brothers. They were at his mercy.

God had given Joseph wisdom for securing food during a time of famine, and because of that wisdom he was able to sustain a nation and a people. His brothers, not knowing Joseph was in an authoritative position, asked to purchase grain. Joseph left their presence and wept bitterly, returning with his heart filled with forgiveness (Gen. 42:24). He said to his brothers, "As for you, you intended to harm me, but God intended it for good, in order to bring it about as it is this day, to save many lives" (Gen. 50:20). He took care of them and forgave them for the evil they had committed against him. Now that is a heart after God. Forgive deeply.

I remember meeting a woman several years ago whose daughter had been brutally beaten, raped, and murdered at just sixteen years old. Ten years after the incident her mother went to the prison where the murderer had been confined for life, and she forgave him and led him to Christ. Forgiveness is never easy, but I can tell you this: forgiveness is much easier than carrying around the poison of unforgiveness. Be willing to forgive. Be quick to forgive. Be certain to forgive.

Shareworthy

The most miserable prison in the world is the prison we make for ourselves when we refuse to show mercy. Our thoughts become shackled, our emotions are chained, the will is almost paralyzed. But when we show mercy, all of these bonds are broken, and we enter into a joyful liberty that frees us to share God's love with others.

—Warren W. Wiersbe[3]

Enjoy Your Present

When you hold a grudge against another person, you will most likely be so wrapped up in that wrong of the past that you cannot enjoy your present. You may think, "It doesn't bother me. I don't even think about them." But here is a test: When speaking to or about a person who has offended you, do you have the need to put in a jab or to one-up them? If so, then you are holding resentment in your heart toward this person. Do you want an unforgiving spirit or health, revenge or peace, hostility or joy, bitterness or contentment? These are just a few examples of how unforgiveness truly affects your life and steals from you, your present, and your future. Forgiveness is the birthplace of your personal freedom: embrace it, walk in it, and live it. Your days will be much brighter.

Joseph, because he was willing to forgive, was propelled into his destiny and was freed from the pain of his past. He was freed from all the hurt, all the rejection, and all the anger that he must have experienced as a young man.

Refusing forgiveness can lead to depression, anxiety, bitterness, resentment, and hostility. Unforgiveness causes you to cut out important relationships in your life. Just look at the life of Joseph. His brothers could have gained significant benefits all throughout their lives by having such a wise and dynamic leader as a brother. Instead they chose the path of hatred, guilt, and shame. Joseph was propelled into his destiny through the hatred and jealousy of his brothers; God had a plan, and it was a good plan.

Forgiveness is a command and a blessing from the Lord. It will free you from negative emotions and the hold others have over you. It will break the ties with a traumatic situation. It will allow you to feel joy again. It will restore your fellowship with God. Forgive because you have been forgiven. Forgive because it better reflects Jesus Christ in you. Forgive because it opens your heart to fellowship with God. Forgive because it frees you from being tied to the pains of the past.

Unforgiveness on the other hand produces in you a seed of bitterness, and that seed can destroy you. It can steal your happiness and contentment in life. When you choose to forgive—and it is a choice—you no longer hold that poison inside your body or soul. You are purified and released when you choose to forgive. Release your offenders, and walk on the path to freedom and wholeness, letting go of the offense.

Shareworthy

Forgiveness is the agent by which God allows healing and joy to come to your inner man.

—Robin Bertram

CLASS REUNION

Recently I had a class reunion coming up. I was excited for the event, and I had fun preparing. I bought a really cute outfit, new shoes, and great accessories, completed with a trip to the salon for my hair, nails, and a pedicure. I have to admit, I was really excited to go. Going back was going home, and I enjoy seeing my old friends.

There was one particular friend I was a bit nervous about seeing. We had been estranged for years, and I didn't know how she would react to seeing me. We had been good friends throughout school, but we had a dispute after school. Words were said, feelings were compromised, and a friendship was destroyed. It's funny how we never feel like we are at fault, and at first this was one of those times. There were some hurtful comments made on her part, but looking back, I know I made a few comments as well. Years after the conflict I wrote her a letter; I took a position of humility and asked her to forgive me for hurting her. I never heard back from her.

I walked into the reunion, and sure enough, she was the first person I saw. As the night went on, I thought it would be nice to just ask how she had been. To my shock and dismay, when I reached out, she jerked her head around and glared at me, responding rather abruptly. As I walked away, I realized that writing the letter years ago had freed my heart from the poison of unforgiveness. I was not being held captive, but she still was. I felt sorry for her. My heart was grieved, but I learned a tremendous lesson on the importance of forgiveness.

As we forgive, we are purified from the defilement that unforgiveness produces. Bitterness is birthed out of a heart that is unwilling to forgive, and the consequence of that bitterness is our own condemnation. It becomes a poison that pollutes everything you do and everything you are. Refuse to be swallowed up in your own bitterness; it is a pool of misery in which you will certainly drown. If you do not forgive, you will live a lifetime of regret. Take a moment right now and think of anyone with whom you might be angry. Do you want to live the most gratifying, fruitful life for the Lord? If so, then go ahead and decide in your heart to release anyone who has let you down or failed you in any way. Just release them. God drops the charges against us as we drop the charges against others. We are forgiven, but we must also forgive.

Extend Forgiveness

An online article published by Johns Hopkins Medicine says: "Whether it's a simple spat with your spouse or long-held resentment toward a family member or friend, unresolved conflict can go deeper than you may realize—it may be affecting your physical health. The good news: Studies have found that the act of forgiveness can reap huge rewards for your health, lowering the risk of heart attack; improving cholesterol levels and sleep; and reducing pain, blood pressure, and levels of anxiety, depression and stress."[4] Isn't it great that science is finally catching up with the truth that has been laid out in Scripture?

Forgiveness is a choice, not a feeling. It is the act of extending grace and mercy. It is the act of releasing an individual. The word in Greek actually means "to send away, to remit, or to cancel."[5] Forgiveness is a means of releasing oneself from bad circumstances by choosing to release the one who has committed an offense. In the government of God we can receive forgiveness only if we extend forgiveness. It is completely analogous to the grace we have been given by God the Father. The Greek words meaning "to let loose" are synonymous with the word for *forgive*. In other words, they are interchangeable. As an individual forgives, he is released from the pain of that negative or harmful situation and is restored in his soul as though it never occurred. He may never forget, but with God's help he can. The pain and hurt associated with the situation no longer rules or dominates his thoughts. People are released as they choose to forgive. Forgiveness is a requirement in the life of a believer; it is not an option. Forgiveness is not denying the other person's responsibility for hurting you, and it doesn't minimize or justify the wrong. It is untying the bonds that hold you captive. Forgiveness is a decision and not a feeling, and we are commanded to do it. When we do, we are guarding our lives from the regret that comes with unforgiveness.

The Lord's Prayer reads, "Forgive us our debts, as we forgive our debtors" (Matt. 6:12). The one small word *as* suggests to the same degree as, to the same extent as, and in the same manner as.[6] Therefore we must forgive.

For several years I carried unforgiveness in my heart. I couldn't understand how such evil that had been directed toward me could go unchecked and uninhibited. I was angry not only with the people who hurt me but also with God. Now, looking back, I think it could possibly have been the root of the illness meant to destroy me.

Please hear me: not all sickness is birthed out of sin, but there are some sins that can produce sickness. We see proof of that from the medical community as well as the Bible. When you have been hurt deeply, in the core of your very being, your natural instinct is to seek revenge. However, revenge does not pay off. Bitterness will pay, but the cost is far greater than you might think, and unforgiveness will steal not only your present but also, if you allow it, your future.

When I was struggling through the illness, those things and people who hurt me so deeply were but a vague shadow in my memory. Those hurts seemed to melt away. The actions of these people did not change; the situation was not resolved, nor did the trauma stop. What changed was my heart. What changed was my desire to live, and to live well. I began to understand how precious life really is and how often we take it for granted. Through this experience I determined in my heart that I would never again allow anyone or anything to steal my joy, peace, and love for life. No matter how hard your situation is, you can release bitterness, resentment, and unforgiveness, and you can love again. Jesus said, "Father, forgive them, for they know not what they do" (Luke 23:34). You can take those defeats and lay them at the foot of the cross once and for all.

Shareworthy

Forgiveness is an act of the will, and the will can function regardless of the temperature of the heart.

—Corrie ten Boom[7]

I watched a precious woman as she decided to forgive her mother and father. Horrific acts had been committed against her, and she had spent years in counseling and on prescription medicine to no avail. She sat in my office, and as we prayed, she raised her head, hands shaking and tears streaming, and said, "I choose to forgive." She was set free from years of depression in that very instant.

Here are eight steps to forgive someone who has hurt you:

1. Realize forgiveness is truly a choice.
2. Trust that you will be freed from the bad experience as you choose to forgive the one who has hurt you.
3. Believe that forgiveness brings reconciliation to God first, and then to the others involved.
4. Understand that unforgiveness does not punish the targeted person, but it does cause you to suffer greatly.
5. Choose to admit the wrong you have committed by holding another in judgment.
6. Ask for forgiveness from God and then from the person involved.
7. Trust God to change your emotions.
8. Release those negative emotions by laying them at the foot of the cross by giving them to God.

No More Regrets

Once you've decided to release all those people you've held captive in your heart, you can begin to fulfill the plans and purposes of God and walk the path God has set before you. You will start to feel the joy of your own salvation and begin to see things from a heavenly perspective. The worries and disappointments that you've been carrying will be lifted from your shoulders. You can walk into your future celebrating the love of the Lord without being chained to your past. You can enjoy life with peace in your heart because you are at peace with God.

The sweet, sweet fellowship with the Lord is worth forgiving those who have hurt you. Trust me. He is worthy of our obedience, our love, and our unbroken fellowship. I refuse to spend my days carrying offenses of any kind against anyone. I have been forgiven; I will forgive.

INTENTIONAL LIVING

- Forgiveness is a choice and decision of your will, so choose to forgive.

- God forgives and forgets, and so should we; do so by capturing those thoughts and replacing them with good thoughts.

- Forgiveness opens communication with God, so as you pray, ask God to reveal any unforgiveness you still may be carrying.

- Unforgiveness will steal from you, your present, and your future; therefore acknowledge the benefits that come to you as you forgive others.

- We are purified and washed as we forgive our offenders; therefore determine to live every day with a forgiving spirit as the offenses come.

- Enjoy your present to the fullest by forgiving people from your past; choose to release those negative emotions by laying them at the foot of the cross.

- Forgiveness unties the bonds that hold us captive; therefore celebrate your freedom from those hurtful experiences.

CHAPTER 9

FAITH FUEL

God's revelation does not need the light of human
genius, the polish and strength of human culture, the
brilliancy of human thought, the force of human brains
to adorn or enforce it; but it does demand the sim-
plicity, the docility, humility, and faith of a child's heart.

—E. M. BOUNDS[1]

G AZING INTO THE mirror one morning while I was battling
the illness, I went to pick up a hairbrush. My right arm
had been very weak, so weak I could barely pick up a glass
of water. I looked at the brush lying on my sink, then I looked into
the mirror, and then again looked at the brush. Tears welled up in
my eyes. I reached for the brush with my left arm. For the first time
I experienced weakness in not only my right arm but also in my
left. "God, help me!" I began to weep profusely as I realized both of
my arms were affected. Questions were whirling through my head:
"God, who is going to brush my hair? How am I going to brush my
teeth? Lord, I need my contacts. How am I going to get them in?"
My heart was pounding. My head was throbbing. Thoughts of death
kept flashing before my face.

I cried out desperately, "No, God! This is not my destiny! I am
supposed to die an old woman. I need to be here. Who is going to
pray for my children? Who is going to help Taylor when she has
her first child? Who is going to be there for my son, Logan, and his
future wife, Kelsey, with their first baby? God, I need to be here to
hold my first grandchild. God, who's going to be here for my nieces
and nephews? God, I love them. I want to be part of their lives. I
need to be here to pray."

My head was bombarded with all the reasons I needed to be here.
I had already been to church and had the elders anoint me with oil

and pray the prayer of faith over me, but at this time my faith was very weak. I envisioned being bedridden and eventually totally paralyzed. Images would come out of nowhere of me being unable to move, unable to speak, and unable to eat. Images of my body being totally useless with me trapped inside ran through my head. The agony was unbearable. I was living a nightmare. These thoughts had to stop, and I had to decide to walk in the faith that I had in my heart.

As I look back over my life, I know that had I not learned to walk in faith at an early age, I would have experienced my greatest life's regrets. I may have not experienced all the miracles I've experienced: my son's healing, my physical and emotional healing, relationships that have been mended, or the joy that has been restored to my life. I certainly would not have known God as intimately as I do now. I hope that through the experiences I am sharing, you will be encouraged to walk a faith-filled life so that you can avoid the pitfalls that may come your way. Without faith my life would have had many different outcomes.

FAITH FUEL

Faith is the fuel for your own miracle. There is great power in faith. I found out just how true that statement really is. For me, going to church for prayer was step one. The Mayo Clinic could give me no hope, and it was time for me to take action. I know this may seem far-fetched to some, but I knew that God was able to heal me. I knew He had given me a vision of the future that did not include being paralyzed and bedridden, or dying an early death. I knew He had given me a promise that my health and finances would not be cut off. The doctors had given me no hope, no meds, and no real answers. They told me, "Go home and wait." I thought, "Wait for what? To die?" They expected things to get progressively worse—I could see it in their eyes. That direction was not acceptable to me.

After returning from the hospital, I ran back into my bedroom, and my knees hit the floor. I cried out again to God. "God, tell me what to do. Tell me how to survive this. I need Your wisdom. Man's wisdom cannot help me. They have nothing to offer me, but I know that You do. Tell me what to do." I sensed in my spirit almost immediately that I was to get every promise of healing that I could find in the Word of God, and that I was to start reading them aloud every day, several times a day. I was to record myself reading those scriptures for the days that I would feel too weak to read them.

God had called me to be a warrior in prayer most of my life. I had learned to battle against powers and principalities, spiritual wickedness in high places, and forces of evil, and now it was imperative that I knew how to pray. You've probably done the same thing at some point in your life if you've walked with the Lord for long—you have hit your knees and cried out for the impossible. That's what I mean, praying for something that you know beyond a shadow of a doubt only God can provide. That's what I did. I battled in prayer and in faith for my health. Regardless of how I felt or what else I might have had to get done, praying was my priority. Many days I was too tired, but I did it anyway. I may not have had enough strength to make my bed, fix breakfast, or even read my Bible, but I made time and found the energy to pray.

How could I possibly pray and ask God to heal me from a potentially fatal disease? There is power in prayer, and prayer that is effective needs faith. All I can tell you is I have spent most of my life reading, studying, and listening to the Word of God. It is through those times of being in His Word that my faith was increased. After all, "faith comes by hearing, and hearing by the word of God" (Rom. 10:17). Without the building of my faith, I could not have had enough faith to pray and ask God to do the miraculous. However, if I accept Genesis 1:1 fully—"In the beginning God created the heavens and the earth"—then I can believe God for anything. Faith can move mountains, and I had a big mountain I needed moved.

Shareworthy

Faith is the fuel for our own miracle, and our miracle may only be as big as our faith.

—Robin Bertram

Put on Your Shield

One day I felt the Lord prompt me to cut off the visions of being an invalid and dying early. I literally would scream, "NO!," when the visions would come. I would say, "I refuse that lie from the devil. I will not be an invalid. I will not be paralyzed. I will not die an early death. I refuse." I want you to know that inside I was trembling, but I also knew that faith-filled proclamations were essential. The hopefulness I had and the certainty I felt were not wishful thinking. I knew in my heart that healing would be forthcoming.

We as believers are commanded to put on the shield of faith (Eph. 6:16). We are to put on faith over a spirit of fear, doubt, or double-mindedness. We are to make a decision to believe the promises of God and to act upon them in faith, claiming them as our own. We are to stand on the promises that are written, refusing to run, hide, or give in to the intimidation of the devil. Believe me, I wanted to run. I wanted to hide from this terrible situation. I wanted to hide from death, but there was no place to run or hide. My only options were to stand or give in to those visions of death. But there was something stirring inside of me that just knew God was bigger, stronger, and more than capable of handling this, no matter the outcome.

Big Faith

Faith is the fuel for our own miracle, and our miracle may only be as big as our faith. I've often wondered what would have happened to me had I not walked in faith when I experienced this illness. What if I had allowed those visions of death to continue planting seeds in my heart? What would have happened had I not read those scriptures two and three times a day? What would have happened if I had just gotten mad at God and given in to my circumstances?

When I was fighting this illness, I knew I had to become stronger in my faith walk. Although I had already witnessed the power of God for healing and miracles in the lives of many others, when it came to my own needs, my faith tended to wane. I could pray for the impossible for everyone except myself, but I persevered in prayer anyway. Romans reads, "Faith comes by hearing, and hearing by the word of God" (Rom. 10:17). Speaking the promises of God was a way to increase my own faith.

Faith that is never exercised is a lost opportunity to experience the miraculous. One thing I am certain of: had I not exercised my faith, I would not be here. Hear me: My words did not heal me. God did. But first I had to exercise what I had confessed and fervently believed for so long.

Shareworthy

Faith is the accepting of what God gives. Faith is the believing what God says. Faith is the trusting to what Jesus has done. Only do this and you are saved, as surely as you are alive!
—Charles Spurgeon [2]

Do Not Wait

My friend, you cannot wait until you are faced with a tragic situation to learn to exercise your faith. You need to learn to exercise your faith now. Not growing in faith may be one of the biggest regrets you will ever experience because of the consequences it may have on your life. You need to learn to walk in faith, fight spiritual battles in faith, and grow in faith. I don't mean to sound super spiritual, but trust me: there will come a time when your faith is tested. I want you to understand now how to better prepare. It may not be your own personal tragedy you have to fight. It may be a difficult experience your child will go through, or perhaps your husband or another loved one. In any case, it is wise to be ready. It is wise to prepare now.

Roller-Coaster Ride

My son had health issues right from birth. When he was born, I told the nurses, "There is something wrong with my baby. He doesn't sound right to me."

They said, "Oh no, honey, you are a nervous mother just as many new mothers are. Not to worry. Your son is fine."

But I knew within me that there was something wrong. I heard it in his cry. I went home with my baby, a bit overwhelmed at being a new mother. His health issues added to this; sometimes Logan would turn blue for no reason at all, and before I could get help, he would begin to breathe again on his own. Those first few months were a roller-coaster ride with him.

It would take approximately five months to find out that he had tracheomalacia, a congenital condition in which the windpipe is floppy and flaccid. At times his windpipe would collapse when he tried to breathe out. He could breathe in but struggled breathing out. Later he developed more breathing issues and had to be on prednisone. We were in and out of the hospital. We never knew when his breathing would become labored and he would have to have a nebulizer treatment. He was a real trouper though. He would pretend it was a toy gun and would run around and try to shoot us with it. We learned to laugh through the darkness and trust God.

Our pediatrician called me at work one day after my mother had taken my son in for an appointment and said, "I'm sorry, Robin, but we need to test him for cystic fibrosis." At that time the prognosis for cystic fibrosis was very poor; children who had it lived to be only eleven or twelve years old. I have to say, I was terrified, but this was a significant turning point in my walk with God. Never before had I cried out to Him in such utter desperation. Never before had I been so totally dependent on Him. Our doctor did the test, and thankfully it was negative for cystic fibrosis. The doctor then sent us to UVA Children's Hospital in Charlottesville, Virginia, concerning an issue with our son's hip. After our initial appointment the doctor came out and said that Logan had Legg-Calvé-Perthes disease, a disease that degrades the femoral cap resulting from a lack of the blood supply to that area. Although there was no way to substantiate it, I was convinced that all the prednisone for Logan's breathing had damaged his hip. We were faced with the real possibility that Logan would need a wheelchair or perhaps a body brace for an extended period of time.

A. W. Tozer said, "Faith is not a conclusion you reach…it's a journey you live."[3]

THE REPORT

Once again I poured my heart out in prayer. I begged. I pleaded. I cried my eyes out. When we received the diagnosis at UVA, the doctors decided to try something new. They did not want to put him in a body cast or a wheelchair; instead they sent us home with an exercise agenda. We were instructed to exercise his hip every night. We did that for six months. When we went back for our six-month checkup, the doctors took a new set of X-rays and, to our doctor's surprise, he was healed. The doctor said, "His healing is miraculous." The cartilage that forms the femoral cap had grown back to such a degree that the only way anyone would ever know my son had once had Legg-Calvé-Perthes would be by looking closely at his X-rays.

FURNACE OF AFFLICTION

Healing faith comes through the furnace of affliction, and it is in that furnace that our self-reliance is burned away. I learned through the experience with my son that if I have to rely on myself or other people, I would be in real trouble. For me this was the proverbial line in the sand; this is when I committed to living my life in such a way as to honor God. I committed to getting to know Him and His Word. I dedicated my time to developing the understanding I needed to walk through this life victoriously, no matter the situation.

Faith is built upon the unwavering expectation that flows from a childlike heart. You cannot pray and ask God for something you do not expect Him to do. How futile would that be? How could you possibly ask for a physical healing if you did not believe that He heals today? The very act of praying is a decision to walk in faith. The very act of asking means that you believe in your heart it is possible. And as the Bible reads, "Without faith it is impossible to please God" (Heb. 11:6). A woman once asked me how I could pray in faith for people who are dying with a terminal illness. My answer was simple: "How could I not?"

Prayer is communication with God, but it is also a perfect expression of our faith in Him and His Word being exercised. Prayer is an important element in exercising faith. So then, how do we pray? Praying for our needs is fine and good, but praying His promises is a whole different thing. Learn to pray the promises found in His Word—in fact, that is how I got through difficult times. I prayed the promises found in the Bible (many of which are included in this book as Pillars of Abundant Living), and they gave me confidence, security, and a mind-set that proved beneficial. The Bible reads, "Whatever you ask in prayer, if you believe, you will receive" (Matt. 21:22). It takes faith to believe something you cannot see. As you read, as you study, and as you find out the true nature of God, then you have ground to stand on and from which to pray. You have something to stand on besides just your wishes. God is never obligated to meet our wants or wishes.

Steps of Faith

Here are five keys to walking out a life of faith as you learn the importance of growing in faith and in the Word of God. Follow these steps to begin a life of faith and to live a life with no regrets.

1. It is written

Your first step in beginning to walk out your life by faith is discovering what is actually written. Life is a faith walk, regardless of your religious belief. Your faith, or lack of faith, will determine how you walk. In other words, you are going to walk in faith or apart from faith. What does the Bible say regarding your situation? What promises can you find to hold onto? What verses can you plant deep in your spirit to combat the thoughts and feelings impacted by your circumstances or your flesh?

Today, as I travel across the country to speak, I find that many women have a very shallow understanding of Scripture. Women are often co-breadwinners and entrepreneurs. They are successful. This is great, but frequently we forget to call on God because we feel so capable. We fail to realize at times that everything we have or have been given is a gift from God, and it can go away quickly. In our independence and lack of understanding we somehow think it is of our own doing that we prosper, leaving God out of the equation.

We do not feel needy or vulnerable because we have learned as women that we can do whatever we set our minds to do. That being said, as I hope I've proven to you through my own personal experience, there will be times when you and I will be completely at the mercy of God. When you begin to understand and properly apply Scripture to your life, you realize that you need God in every aspect of your life. Understanding how to apply Scripture comes by revelation and inspiration of the Holy Spirit; the natural mind cannot understand the depth and complexity of such wondrous things.

2. Revelation

The second step in growing in faith is growing in revelation and understanding. The Word quoted has little or no value if you do not understand what it is actually saying. Grab your Bible, pray, and ask the Holy Spirit to teach you things you do not know. He will. He will bring great revelation as you submit to Him.

I remember many years ago battling with anxiety to the point of having panic attacks. One day, after refusing medication prescribed by my medical doctor, I grabbed my Bible and shouted aloud, "I know my answers are here, and I'm going to find them." That is one of the best decisions I ever made. My other option would have been to take antianxiety meds and sleepwalk my way through life. I have a bachelor of science in psychology, so hear me: I know there are times that you may need those meds. And that's OK. But I knew that for me such a decision would be the worst thing I could do.

After I shouted out to God, I sat down, and almost immediately the Holy Spirit started teaching me how to apply Scripture to my situation. For example, as I read, "Perfect love casts out fear," it was as though a light bulb went on in my head and heart (1 John 4:18). I gained the understanding that fear was not part of my personality as I had thought, but it was an enemy that needed to go. Through a heartfelt prayer the spirit of fear left me, and so did the anxiety that had plagued my life from childhood.

Reading Scripture, believing it is for you, and gaining the understanding to adequately apply it are steps to growing in faith. But you can't stop there. You can have Scripture and an adequate understanding, yet still fall short by refusing to act upon it.

3. Walk it out

Now that you have the scripture that applies to your life and an adequate understanding of what that scripture actually means and that it is for you, the third step is to walk it out. We as believers are instructed to walk by the Spirit, not by the flesh (Gal. 5:16). Walking by the Spirit and not the flesh means walking in faith. It's allowing yourself to be influenced not by what is seen but by a knowing in your spirit. Our flesh screams at us. It is constantly seeking attention and craving things that are not good for us. Our spirit on the other hand has been renewed. We are a new creature in Christ (2 Cor. 5:17). Therefore we are obligated to walk as Christ walked.

Walking by faith is not a big denial game. I'm not suggesting you act as though you do not have a real problem, but I am saying that you must not let the problem have you: It is not your cancer. It is not your heart disease. It is not your MS. It is not your diabetes. I refused to take ownership of the thing that was meant to destroy me; it was an enemy, and I refused to call it anything more. I didn't deny having an issue. Instead I determined in my heart that this battle with illness would not kill me. It was an enemy, and treating it in any other way would have been counterproductive. Whatever the challenge you are facing, do not let it define you. You are victorious in Christ Jesus, no matter the severity of the battle.

4. Victory

The fourth step in this process is seeing your situation from the viewpoint of victory. See past your current situation, stand on the promises written, and gaze into the day when they will actually manifest in your life. Walking in faith and praying by faith means having eyes to see past the situation, believing that with God all things are possible (Matt. 19:26). It is walking and praying from a position of victory instead of from a position of defeat. Have certainty that God is looking out for you from an eternal perspective, and be willing to trust in His leadership. God works all things together for the good of those who love Him and are called according to His purpose (Rom. 8:28); hence His leadership is right and safe.

5. Reject the lies of the enemy

The fifth step in learning to walk out your faith is to reject the lies of Satan that stand in opposition to the written Word of God. Walking in faith is a moment-by-moment decision. It means rejecting the tormenting thoughts, visions, and conclusions coming your way and replacing them with the promise of abundant life that Jesus came to give us (John 10:10). It means seeing with eyes of promise that God has exalted His name and His Word above all things. There is nothing more reliable or more powerful than His name and His Word, and when we begin to grasp the importance of that fact, we can then trust in His uncompromising truth.

Pillar of Abundant Living

For whoever is born of God overcomes the world, and the victory that overcomes the world is our faith.

—1 John 5:4

WALKING IN THE SPIRIT

Walking in the Spirit is the same as allowing the Word of Christ to richly dwell in you (Col. 3:16) and following the Holy Spirit's lead. Spiritual things must be spiritually discerned. Man, in his human thinking, cannot grasp spiritual things. Therefore relying on the Holy Spirit is fundamental to walking in the Spirit. Herein lies the concern. Walking in the Spirit requires leadership of the Holy Spirit and oftentimes goes in direct opposition to your natural mind. Hear me: walking in the Spirit does not mean that you are to act wackily or irresponsibly.

The leadership of the Holy Spirit is always going to be lined up with Scripture. Herein lies your test and measurement. It is the way that you are to gauge your own hearing. The leadership of the Holy Spirit will always be in line with His nature, His character, and the written Word of God. There will never be a time when you will be instructed to do something that will bring harm to you or to others, or when you are told to do something contrary to Scripture. The Holy Spirit is our Comforter and Teacher. He is our gift giver. He gives us good gifts for the edification of our own spirit as well as for the strength and building of the church. We are to be led by the Holy Spirit if we are truly God's sons and daughters (Rom. 8:14). The leadership of the Holy Spirit will always be to further the kingdom of God and the purposes of God for your life and the life of your family.

A LIFE OF PURPOSE

The only way to walk through this life with any real meaning and purpose is to walk in faith. Perhaps you're in a situation right now that you cannot see past. You look, but the future, or at least a good future, is not on the horizon. Hold on. God has a good plan for you even if you cannot see it presently.

The illness I struggled with stripped away my vision, and I struggled through it. I remember days of total bleakness when I could not see a good future. The days were long, dark, and painful. As Proverbs says, without vision the people perish (Prov. 29:18). I understood the dangers of remaining in that place, so I began to pray and ask God to give me a vision of my future again. It did not happen instantly, but gradually the Lord began to give me hope and a future. He restored my spiritual eyesight, and I began to see again. As I walked in faith, expecting to have a future, God began to restore my sight and my dreams. He can do the same for you today. Reach out to Him and allow Him to restore to you all that has been lost. Begin today to grow in faith by growing in the Word.

A faith-filled life is a life lived with no regrets. When living a life of faith, your decisions will come from a place of prayer, trust in His Word, and guidance of the Holy Spirit. Those decisions will always honor God and honor man. They will be decisions based on the Word of God instead of our weak-willed emotions and skewed attitudes. It will be a life well lived. It will be filled with peace knowing that you are living in such a way that pleases God. Truly God has all the right answers in His Word, and if we will submit to Him and walk in a way that pleases Him, there will be no room for regret. Live well, and live out your faith. Your ultimate victory has already been determined.

Pillar of Abundant Living

For I know the plans that I have for you, says the LORD, plans for peace and not for evil, to give you a future and a hope. Then you shall call upon Me, and you shall come and pray to Me, and I will listen to you. You shall seek Me and find Me, when you shall search for Me with all your heart.

—Jeremiah 29:11–13

INTENTIONAL LIVING

- Fuel your own miracles with faith.
- Feed your spirit and grow in your faith through dedication to reading the Word of God.
- Put on your shield of faith to fight against doubt and uncertainty.

- Ask the Holy Spirit to bring greater revelation and understanding.
- Learn to walk in the Spirit as you learn to follow the leading of the Holy Spirit.
- Pray and walk from a position of victory instead of from a position of defeat.
- Actively cast down the lies of Satan.
- Learn to exercise your faith in the small day-to day decisions because faith that is never exercised is a lost opportunity to experience the miraculous.

PART III

LEAVE A LEGACY

CHAPTER 10

SECOND CHANCES

At times God puts us through the discipline of darkness to teach us to heed Him. Song birds are taught to sing in the dark, and we are put into the shadow of God's hand until we learn to hear Him...Watch where God puts you into darkness, and when you are there keep your mouth shut. Are you in the dark just now in your circumstances, or in your life with God? Then remain quiet....When you are in the dark, listen, and God will give you a very precious message for someone else when you get into the light.

—OSWALD CHAMBERS[1]

I REMEMBER SITTING IN darkness. After my initial doctor's visit, when I understood what I was up against, my life just seemed to stop. Everything was put on hold, and I was surrounded by darkness. My thoughts were consumed daily with the reason it all was happening. Why was I sick? Why was I facing an incurable, untreatable, fatal illness? Why was my life being cut short? I sat in darkness with my questions.

After fighting through the darkness, I learned something: God gives us a very precious message for others when we go through such tremendous difficulties. It is in the second chances of life that we learn our greatest lessons. What message did God give me for others? God taught me through my raging storm that He is more than sufficient, that the days He has given me are to be treasured, that my heart is to be pure, and that my love is to be freely poured out to others. I learned to appreciate the small things, rejoice in truth, and celebrate His goodness day by day. I learned to love more deeply, speak kindly, and forgive freely even when others may not be willing to forgive me. He taught me to live my life in such a way as to have no regrets by living the precepts found in the Bible in every decision I make. "No regrets" means living a well-lived life, a life that honors God and people, a life that leaves a godly legacy. It means constantly abiding in Him, being fruitful for His kingdom, and accomplishing the work that we have been given to do for Him.

Ricky Jackson had no regrets. He was the man charged with murdering Harold Franks outside a convenience store in 1975 and wrongly imprisoned for thirty-nine years. The only eyewitness to the shooting, a young boy twelve years of age at the time, lied about being at the scene of the murder when he was actually a block away. The misidentification stole nearly forty years of Mr. Jackson's life. When the eyewitness recanted his story, Mr. Jackson stated that he had no ill will for the man, but he was thankful the man was brave enough to recant his testimony. Ricky Jackson was given a second chance in life, and it was one he well deserved. He can now live as a regular citizen, free to go wherever he chooses, whenever he chooses. "Just because you're in prison, you don't have to be a prisoner," Jackson told reporters. "You got to be a man, and you got to get yourself together, no matter what the circumstances are, and you got to press forward. You know you're innocent and got to keep fighting." His humility, his strength, and his willingness to forgive speak to the kind of man he really is, and life is a little sweeter now that he has been given a second chance.[2]

Shareworthy

We are not responsible for the circumstances we are in, but we are responsible for the way we allow those circumstances to affect us; we can either allow them to get on top of us or we can allow them to transform us into what God wants us to be.

—Oswald Chambers[3]

GOD OF SECOND CHANCES

God is the God of second chances. He longs to help us live the best life we can live and fulfill our fullest potential in Him. He wants us to be fruitful for His kingdom and intimately dependent on Him for our every need, walking in the boldness and confidence of His Son. He gave each one of us who is born again a second chance. He gave us a do-over; all our past sins have been wiped away, our lives have been restored to fellowship with Him, and we have been given the greatest second chance to live and to live well.

Even with this you and I often need something to shake us up, to wake us out of our slumber, and to put a fire under our feet so that we will move. Sometimes we wake up too late, only to realize that what we once had, we no longer have. We cry out to God, "Oh God, I wish I could do it all over again." We wake up and realize that our youth is gone, our health is gone, or our family is gone. Whatever the loss, we realize that God had given us a chance for a great life, but we took things for granted or made some wrong decisions, and now that chance is gone.

I encourage you to make the necessary changes to live a life worth living: evaluate your life, identify those things that need to change, and make those changes. Grow in spiritual maturity and learn to walk in the Spirit and in faith. I encourage you to walk in the fruit of the Holy Spirit: love, joy, peace, patience, faithfulness, kindness, goodness, gentleness, and self-control. I encourage you to live for Jesus Christ today because tomorrow is not promised.

Shareworthy

Any step away from the cross is a step in the wrong direction.

—Greg Laurie [4]

THE WRONG DIRECTION

Years ago I was supposed to meet my husband, Ken, in Lexington, Kentucky. I started out in Virginia and drove four and a half hours only to find I was in the wrong state. I stopped at a gas station to pick up a map. The attendants there were quite amused as they explained that I was desperately off course. I called Ken to let him know that I would be about five hours late, but I did not share with him the reason for my delay for years. If I had taken the time to find out where I was actually supposed to be going instead of assuming I knew the way, I would have saved myself about ten hours of driving time and a whole lot of embarrassment for making such a big mistake. We laugh about it now, but at the time it was not that funny.

Have you ever started out on a trip and thought you knew where you were going but ended up going the wrong way? Or perhaps you thought for sure that you knew the way but really did not and were too proud to stop for directions. There is an Old Testament servant and prophet of God who thought he knew the way to go, and he ended up in a really bad place. Jonah of Nineveh, out of sheer disobedience to God, went the wrong way. He knew the right way, but he chose the wrong way. That's what we do far too often.

Jonah was a man on the run from God. He was a prophet with a prophetic word to give to a specific people in a specific place at a specific time. So what did he do? He ran thousands of miles in the opposite direction. Have you ever felt that way? Have you ever thought that you just cannot do what has been asked of you? Perhaps you know the plans God has for your life, but you just keep putting it off. Well, you, Jonah, and I have all been in the same boat.

Jonah set out thinking he would determine his own course because he thought he knew what was best for his life. He headed west to Tarshish instead of east to Nineveh. According to today's best speculations, Tarshish was where Spain is now and nearly three thousand miles away from Nineveh.[5] The Lord told him to arise and go to Nineveh (Jonah 1:2); this message had an implied now, as in *right now*.[6] Not "*If you feel like it, Jonah.*" Not, "*If it fits into your schedule, Jonah.*" It was a clear word: "Get up, go to Nineveh" (Jonah 1:2).

Jonah went in the wrong direction by choice. God sent Jonah on a divine mission with divine direction and clarity, but he chose the very opposite direction (Jonah 1:3). The story is the message. It is about a prophet on the run, a God who cares for those who do not acknowledge Him, a fish used as a tool of judgment, and a pagan king who would turn around a whole nation through prayer and fasting. It's a story of repentance and restoration along with a message of miraculous deliverance, not just of an individual but also of an entire nation. It is also a beautiful picture of our merciful God giving a second chance at life and in ministry to those who are undeserving, as we all are.

Jonah ran because God wanted him to warn the harsh Assyrians in Nineveh so they would repent and not perish, but because Jonah was a nationalist who had great love for his people, he wanted them to perish. They were a ruthless people who were archenemies of Israel. Jonah had total disregard for their welfare (Jonah 4:1–2). As Jonah was on the ship headed in the opposite direction, God sent a storm to get him back on the right path. Jonah told the men to throw him overboard because he was the reason for the storm. They did, and Jonah ended up in the belly of a fish. (See Jonah 1–2.) If only he had chosen to follow the path laid out for him, he may have avoided the near-death experience altogether.

Pillar of Abundant Living

When He had called the people to Him, with His disciples, He said to them, "If any man would come after Me, let him deny himself and take up his cross and follow Me."

—Mark 8:34

Jonah, just like most of us, had to hit rock bottom before he woke up and obeyed the call of God on his life. At times God has to send a storm to get us to go in the right direction. We may need to be near death before we look up, repent, and turn from our sin. Jonah had three days in the belly of the fish, and from that place of death he cried out to God, repented of his disobedience, and was given a second chance at life. The fish spat him up on the sand, and he went forth to complete the mission given him.

Pillar of Abundant Living

Trust in the LORD with all your heart, and lean not on your own understanding; in all your ways acknowledge Him, and He will direct your paths.

—Proverbs 3:5–6

INCOMPLETE MISSION

Seven years ago God gave me a mission: write a book that would encourage families who were faced with a loved one going through long-term or terminal illness. I knew it was an assignment from the Lord. I remember the day; I remember the place; I remember whom I was with and where I was. I was at the altar of a church in Burlington, North Carolina, and the Lord gave me clear direction just as He did Jonah. The book sat on my computer for years with little effort put toward completing it. I then found myself with the very real possibility of needing long-term care and my family needing the very comfort I was to write about. I learned a crucial life lesson—if God says to do something, do it. You do not wait. You do not delay until a more convenient time, and you do not put it off. You do it. Would I have had to go through this experience if I had written the book when God instructed me to do so? I can't say for sure, but in my heart of hearts I believe I may have avoided this tremendous fire. The potential of my facing death gave me the incentive to share with others the lessons I learned from my father's life as well as my own. My father's life was well lived for the Lord and void of regrets, and he did complete his mission. What a tremendous lesson. Just like Jonah, I was near death. Just like Jonah, I had no way of escape. Just like Jonah, I was entangled in the pit of darkness, and I knew that it was in God's hands alone. Only His mercy and loving-kindness could get me through.

Once Jonah saw his need to walk in obedience to God, and once he truly repented of his rebellious ways, then he was delivered from the pit of death. To be fruitful for the Lord, we are to confess our shortcomings, our sins, and our rebellion with complete sincerity. Delayed obedience is disobedience. Partial obedience is disobedience. Jonah, through his willingness to acknowledge his sin of rebellion before the Lord, was going forth to complete his intended mission and be fruitful for the Lord.

You do not want to wait until you have an encounter with devastation as Jonah and I did before you live a life fully submitted to the will of the Lord. If you do, you are guaranteeing a life filled with remorse, guilt, regret, and disappointment. We cannot be satisfied in our inner spirit man while walking in rebellion against God. Things may look good on the outside, but inside, where it really matters, there will be a big black hole that needs to be filled.

As believers we are to walk in a manner worthy of the Lord (Col. 1:10). We are to walk in a way that is fully pleasing to Him. We have His Spirit dwelling in us, so we are not powerless against sin. We are empowered over sin, and it no longer has dominion over us (Rom. 6:14). If you look back at your life, which I strongly encourage you to do, you will see there is an evident connection between sin and regret. Nearly everything that causes regret is in some way attached to sin, a sinful lifestyle, or an act of defiance against God. How do you live a life that is regret-free? Be obedient to God's will, His Word, and His guidance in your life. It's never too late to make these changes.

Pillar of Abundant Living

You will know them by their fruit. Do men gather grapes from thorns, or figs from thistles? Even so, every good tree bears good fruit. But a corrupt tree bears evil fruit.

—Matthew 7:16–17

Jesus told a parable about a man who had a fig tree in his vineyard, but it would bear no fruit. So the man told the keeper of the

vineyard that for three years he had looked for the plant to produce fruit, but it had not; therefore he told him to cut it down. The
vine keeper asked to let him fertilize it and dig around it first, and
after that, if it would not produce, then he would cut it down (Luke
13:6–9). The takeaway is this: Jesus expects us to produce fruit. He
expects us to be fruitful in character. He expects us to be fruitful
in our relationships. He expects us to be fruitful for His kingdom
work. Are you fulfilling these expectations?

ABIDING

As believers we are to have a beautiful inner disposition along with
a gentle and quiet spirit. The Word tells us that these are precious
in the sight of God (1 Pet. 3:4). These attributes come from abiding
in Christ. It is through abiding in Him that we are fruitful for His
kingdom and live a life that pleases Him. Do you abide in Him?
Does He lead you and guide you daily?

Pillar of Abundant Living

Abide in Me, and I in you. As the branch cannot bear
fruit of itself unless it abides in the vine, so neither can
you unless you abide in Me.

—John 15:4, NASB

We are to abide in Him, knowing that apart from Him we can
do nothing. The word *abide* infers to stay in one place, to dwell, or
to remain.[7] We are instructed in Scripture to let the Word that
we heard in the beginning abide in us; if we will do that, then we
will abide in the Son and in the Father (1 John 2:24). We are to
abide in love to live in the light and not stumble around in the darkness (v. 10). We are not to love the world or the things of the world
because if the love of the world is in us, the love of the Father is
not (v. 15). How powerful. If we are going to abide in Christ and be
fruitful for His kingdom, then we are to rid ourselves of the desires

of the flesh, the desires of the eyes, and the pride of life because such things do not come from the Father but from the world.

If we are going to abide, then we must practice righteousness by taking the commands and precepts of the Bible each and every day in every situation and determining to live those out. Through such practice our righteousness becomes stronger and becomes an ongoing, habitual aspect of our character. If we abide in Him and love Him, then the Word tells us that we will keep His commands (John 14:15). We will abide in love because God is love, and those who abide in love, abide in Him. Abiding in Him is the key to being fruitful for His kingdom.

Jesus said, "This is to my Father's glory, that you bear much fruit, showing yourselves to be my disciples" (John 15:8, NIV). Are you bearing fruit, living your life with love, peace, joy, patience, kindness, goodness, faithfulness, gentleness, and self-control? We are to reflect the character of God. These virtues are characteristic of Jesus and are the fruit of the Holy Spirit (Gal. 5:22–23). As believers we are to live them out, walk in them, and grow in them daily.

You may ask, "How do I walk in them?" You walk in them by refusing to fulfill the desires of the flesh because it will lead us astray. Our flesh will cause us to overreact, run from those things we are to do for the Lord, and become complacent in our walk with God. The flesh is constantly at war with the spirit; it wants what it wants and gets very ugly when it does not get what it wants. Bring your flesh into submission. The Word tells us that those who belong to Christ have crucified the flesh with all its passions and desires (Gal. 5:24). We have to actively say no to our flesh, and we can do that. We can say no to the flesh and yes to the spirit. The one you feed will get stronger.

God leads us if we will allow Him to do so. He wants us to follow. Fruitful living is determined by our willingness to walk where God tells us to walk and to do what He tells us to do when He tells us to do it. A life well lived is one that is lived for His glory and one that obeys His clear direction and commands. Trust me, not doing so will bring about regret. On the other hand, doing so brings a life of contentment and fulfillment.

Pillar of Abundant Living

But the fruit of the Spirit is love, joy, peace, patience, kindness, goodness, faithfulness, gentleness, self-control; against such things there is no law.

—Galatians 5:22–23, ESV

DIRECTIONALLY CHALLENGED

My friend came for a visit from Tennessee. We went out to lunch and were on our way home, and we were laughing like little girls as we reminisced about all the wonderful times we used to have when I hosted events in Nashville. I was just miles from my home, but during my battle against illness, I could not figure out what street to take to get home. My mind was so confused, I could not think. We drove around in circles for what seemed like forever because even though we were only five miles or so from my home, I could not find my way. How scary is that? Listen, this disease was trying to destroy me, and at that very moment I felt like it was winning. My friend was very kind and kept me calm. We laughed about it and finally it came to me where I was to turn to make it back home.

Perhaps you feel lost and can't seem to find your way. God has the right path for you to walk on, if you will allow it. He will lead you through your life and your assignments and then safely lead you home.

Shareworthy

Every person who will learn the right way, and who will then continue diligently to follow that right way, is absolutely certain in time to possess great riches and all attending blessings.

—Joseph Franklin Rutherford [8]

SECOND CHANCE TO LIVE

When I tell you that God gave me a second chance at life, I really mean He gave me a second chance at life. Psalm 30:2 is the perfect demonstration of what God did in my life: "LORD my God, I called to you for help, and you healed me" (NIV). I am eternally grateful. When I came out victoriously, I had changed. I got to the other side and wanted to better serve my living Savior and reach more people for the sake of the gospel. I came out wanting to share my faith with anyone who would listen. I determined in my heart that I would live a life that fully pleases God because in the big picture it's the only thing that really matters.

God gave Mr. Jackson a second chance. God gave Jonah a second chance. God gave the city of Nineveh a second chance. And God gave me a second chance. He is the God of second chances. Perhaps you need a second chance too. If so, be quick to obey, quick to follow, and quick to commit to growing in your walk with the Lord. Going in the wrong direction will surely result in great disappointment and lots of regrets. Once you realize you've been walking away from God's plans and purposes for your life, you can simply make the choice to turn around and go in the right direction.

As you take your second chance, keep this Charles Spurgeon quote in mind: "My soul has learned yet more fully than ever, this day, that there is no satisfaction to be found in earthly things—God alone can give rest to my spirit."[9]

INTENTIONAL LIVING

- Take full responsibility for where you are and have been.
- Grow in your spiritual walk and learn to abide in Him.
- Be quick to obey the Lord in all things.
- Determine to serve Him to your fullest capabilities.

- Choose to be mindful of the purpose and timing of your mission.
- Change what needs to be changed, and forget what cannot be changed.
- Ask God to lead you in the right direction and expect to hear from Him.

CHAPTER 11

PAYING IT FORWARD

Do all the good you can. By all the means you
can. In all the ways you can. In all the places
you can. At all the times you can. To all the
people you can. As long as ever you can.

—JOHN WESLEY [1]

MY SON LOGAN came to me with a demand one Christmas. Logan, who was only eleven, told me that he wanted me to do something for him and that I would have to agree to it. I of course told him that I would not agree with anything until I at least heard his request. He proceeded by saying, "OK, Mom, but you still have to agree to it because it is what I really want you to do." Now he had my attention. Logan was the sweetest child—quiet, studious, kindhearted, and compassionate. He didn't demand or even frequently ask for things as a child. He said, "Mom, I want you to take all that you would normally get for me at Christmas and put it toward a family in need." He continued, "And Mom, you can't get me anything for Christmas. That would be cheating. I want to give it all."

"Logan," I said, "do you understand what you are asking of me? That is very generous of you to give away your entire Christmas, but I'm not sure that you are thinking this through. How are you going to feel on Christmas when there is nothing under the tree for you?"

Logan replied, "Mom, I'll be fine, and this is very important, and I really want you to do this for me."

Christmas Eve came that year, and our family loaded up the Suburban with Christmas for a family we knew who would otherwise have no Christmas. There were bikes, pajamas, bedding, towels, games, toothbrushes, clothes, toys, and so on. We went to the family's home and distributed all their Christmas gifts—beautifully wrapped, tagged, and tied up with ribbons and bows. The family was very grateful, but the real blessing was ours. My children got an appreciation for what they had been given when they walked into this family's house. It was all I could do to hold back the tears— tears of joy because my son had insisted on being a blessing in someone else's life even when it would cost him something. It was a big sacrifice for such a young boy, giving up his entire Christmas. I remember as we left their home, I looked at my son's face, and he beamed with the sweetest smile of contentment. It would be a day we all would remember. How dare I hesitate to grant such a beautiful act of paying it forward!

Shareworthy

God doesn't bless us just to make us happy;
He blesses us to make us a blessing.

—Warren W. Wiersbe[2]

GRACE ABOUNDS

God is able to bless you abundantly so that you will have everything you need to abound in good work. Paying it forward does not mean lack; it means abundance. Paying it forward does not take away; it gives. Paying it forward is not man's idea; it's God's. This is a spiritual principle that applies to our finances, the use of our spiritual gifts and talents, our godly wisdom and advice, and anything we have in our possession to help another. When we give, we get back in greater measure. We are to be a conduit for the love of God to freely flow through us. It's what we hold onto that we can never really have. That being said, the motive for giving must not be to get back.

We can never pay back God for the good He has done for us. Make no mistake: salvation is a free gift. God gave His Son to cover our debt, and we can never pay Him back for His free gift of grace. Grace and truth have been realized through Jesus Christ. Therefore grace cannot be paid back; it is a free gift of God. Good deeds will never get you into heaven or in some way pay God back for His gracious sacrifice. Good deeds do not make you commendable before God; the acceptance of His Son as your personal Savior does. However, believers have a responsibility; we have been blessed, and we are to be a blessing. We are to be a blessing and to give in order to reflect the love of God that we've already been given. We pay it forward.

BE A BLESSING

Be a blessing and pay it forward because you have been given blessings. In chapter 22 of the Book of Genesis we see that Abraham had to make a decision to be obedient to God or not. God told him to go to Mount Moriah and sacrifice his son Isaac as a burnt offering. Without hesitation Abraham made all the preparations and headed to the place of sacrifice with Isaac by his side. Abraham reached the top of the mountain, built an altar, placed his son on the altar, and lifted his knife in the air to do as he had been commanded. In that exact moment an angel of the Lord called to him and told him not to do it. God was testing Abraham to see if he would give up his most treasured possession, his son, and he passed the test. Because Abraham had obeyed the instruction of the Lord, God would bless him and would make his descendants numerous:

> By Myself I have sworn, says the LORD, because you have done this thing, and have not withheld your son, your only son, I will indeed bless you and I will indeed multiply your descendants as the stars of the heavens and as the sand that is on the seashore. Your descendants will possess the gate of their enemies. Through your offspring all the nations of the earth will be blessed, because you have obeyed My voice.
> —GENESIS 22:16–18

Take note of that last sentence: through Abraham's offspring "all the nations of the earth will be blessed"—Jesus Christ being that seed. Through Jesus the world would be blessed (Acts 3:25–26).

You can see the pay it forward concept in the first book of the Bible when God promised to bless Abraham so that he and his offspring would in turn be a blessing. God invented the concept of paying it forward long before man coined the term. He gave clear direction in His Word that we are to be a blessing because we have been blessed. (See 2 Corinthians 9:8–9.) Every blessing comes from God: "Every good gift and every perfect gift is from above" (James 1:17). All good things come from God, even those blessings that we acquire and pass on originate from God. We should not take the credit for passing on good. No, it all belongs to God. Out of His fullness we have all received grace—a free gift given. Grace abounds. Therefore God through His Word has instructed us to excel in the grace of giving.

Pillar of Abundant Living

Since you excel in so many ways—in your faith, your gifted speakers, your knowledge, your enthusiasm, and your love from us—I want you to excel also in this gracious act of giving.

—2 Corinthians 8:7, NLT

Sow Generously

Paul wrote, "He who sows sparingly will also reap sparingly, and he who sows bountifully will also reap bountifully" (2 Cor. 9:6). How are you sowing today, sparingly or generously? God tells us in His Word that if we honor Him with our wealth, our barns will be filled with plenty and our vats will overflow with new wine, which simply means we will have more than enough (Prov. 3:9–10). We know this, yet we fail at times to practice the principles in His Word. We sometimes fear that we may not have enough for ourselves and our families, or perhaps we are just plain stingy. Sometimes we play judge and decide others don't deserve an act of kindness, so we do not sow into their lives.

But we now know this is how we are to live. We are to forgive because we have been forgiven. We are to give because we've received. We are to love because God first loved us.

The Word of God tells us, "Be not deceived. God is not mocked.

For whatever a man sows, that will he also reap" (Gal. 6:7). We see in this one verse that we've been given a warning and an encouragement. God is not mocked. He knows our hearts, our motives, and our actions. Therefore there is no need to pretend. You will get what you give, good or bad. Sowing starts with a single seed. When a seed is planted in the ground, after it has had time to germinate, it will grow and produce fruit, and in that fruit there are even more seeds. The seeds you sow today will one day become a harvest; sow seeds of resentment, bitterness, hatred, sin, or discord, and it will come back to you just as seeds of forgiveness, kindness, love, joy, and righteousness will be returned to you. You can make decisions that will bring about a life of regret or a life filled with peace, love, and joy. Choose the seeds you sow today wisely.

MULTIPLYING EFFECT

A grain of wheat must first fall to the earth and die before it will bear much fruit (John 12:24). The Word says, "But he who received seed on the good ground is he who hears the word and understands it, who indeed bears fruit. Some produce a hundred, sixty, or thirty times what was sown" (Matt. 13:23). There is a multiplying effect of your seed; one seed will bring forth many more seeds and much more fruit. You will get a harvest of what you have been sowing. God is a God of multiplication. He can take a little and make a lot.

Pillar of Abundant Living

Truly, truly I say to you, unless a grain of wheat falls into the ground and dies, it remains alone. But if it dies, it bears much frit. He who loves his life will lose it. And he who hates his life in this world will keep it for eternal life. If anyone serves Me, he must follow Me. Where I am, there will My servant be also. If anyone serves Me, the Father will honor him.

—John 12:24-26

This multiplying effect can be seen in more than just seeds and harvests. Look at the times Jesus fed thousands. One such story is recorded in John 6. Jesus took just a few loaves and fish given freely by a little boy, gave thanks for them, and then started passing it out, "as much as they wanted" (John 6:11). Everyone ate their fill because the Lord multiplied the food.

While taking my children to school one morning, I heard a radio program about a woman who had been on a plane. God told her to share the vision for her ministry with the woman seated next to her. The woman argued with God because she did not want to do it, but eventually she went to the bathroom and prayed. While she was praying, God asked her, "Will you share your lunch?" Remember the little boy who had only a small lunch but gave it to the disciples? God took what little he had and multiplied the fish and the bread and fed five thousand with it. The woman said, "Yes, God, I will share my lunch." She went out and shared her story and her vision for ministry, which was to bring improvement to the educational system. The woman in the seat by her happened to be one of the top decision makers in the US Department of Education, who then asked if she would come on board as an adviser. God has big plans, and they are usually much bigger than we can think or imagine.

That day, after listening to the radio program, I was praying while driving home, and I felt the Lord prompting me to go to Subway. The Holy Spirit sometimes led me to do things that seemed out of the ordinary, but I trusted His leadership. I drove there, thinking perhaps there would be someone there who needed prayer. When I got to the restaurant, I did not see anything and thought I must have made a mistake. I purchased a sandwich for lunch, got back in my car, and drove home. I was sitting in my family room and began to open my bag when I heard in my spirit, "Robin, will you share your lunch?" I looked down at my little bag, and inside was a sandwich of bread and fish. My knees hit the floor and I cried out, "Yes, God, yes. I will share my lunch." I spent that afternoon on my knees in prayer, humbled and astounded at His love, His leadership, and His grace. Now that may sound crazy to you, but for me it was a gracious, loving call of the Lord, asking me to use the little I had for His glory, and it still brings tears to my eyes. It was a simple, yet powerful reminder that He would take my little amount and make it much.

So I ask you, "Will you share your lunch?" Whatever little you have, God is the great multiplier, and He will turn it into much more than it could ever be if left in your own hands.

THE PROMISE OF GENEROSITY

"Give, and it will be given to you" (Luke 6:38). Generosity has a blessing attached to it. The Word of God says that a generous man will be prosperous and the man that waters will be watered himself (Prov. 11:25). The concept of reaping and sowing is threaded throughout numerous passages in the Bible. We will be enriched in every way for the generosity we display. If we give to the poor, we are lending to the Lord. In fact, Proverbs states that if we give to the poor, we will not have lack (Prov. 28:27). When we bless others, God will take care of our needs. Generosity has many rewards attached to it, and we don't want to miss them.

Shareworthy

God has given us two hands—one to receive with and the other to give with. We are not cisterns made for hoarding; we are channels made for sharing.

—Billy Graham[3]

My daughter, Taylor, knows and lives this principle. Taylor has brought great joy into my life. She is smart and thoughtful and beautiful. She is a natural leader. But most importantly she is compassionate. She has a heart of gold, and she gets it legitimately. My mother had the gift of giving, and my daughter inherited that same gift. My mother would give the shirt off her back to someone in need, and so would my daughter. Taylor helps others. She has shared her clothes with her friends for special events. She has helped students go on cross-cultural projects through her church and has supported friends who were going abroad to minister as missionaries. She has bought lunches for her classmates who didn't have money to buy their own. She has organized fund-raisers for people in need. Oftentimes she will pay for a meal for a complete stranger in a restaurant out of the kindness of her heart. She is the kind of daughter every mom would be proud of. Christ shines through her and through her generosity. Her heart is for giving to those less fortunate. We can all learn from that kind of heart and attitude.

Giving from the heart is a great display of the love of Christ in operation. You will never regret showing acts of kindness. You will never regret living a life that brings joy to others. You will never regret helping to bear another's burdens because in this you are fulfilling the law of Christ. You will never regret helping those who are less fortunate. How has God blessed you? How can you pay it forward? Do it for your own spiritual growth and maturity as well as to honor God.

Pillar of Abundant Living

Give, and it will be given to you. They will pour into your lap a good measure—pressed down, shaken together, and running over. For by your standard of measure it will be measured to you in return.

—Luke 6:38, NASB

We will have all we need for any good work. God will take your little and multiply it and enlarge the harvest that results from your righteousness, and you will grow richer and cause others to give thanks to God. What a tremendous promise we have when we pay it forward. Did you see that? God supplies the seed, God multiplies the seed, God enlarges the harvest of that seed, and you are blessed in your giving.

Shareworthy

In all of my years of service to my Lord, I have discovered a truth that has never failed and has never been compromised. That truth is that it is beyond the realm of possibilities that one has the ability to out-give God. Even if I give the whole of my worth to Him, He will find a way to give back to me much more than I gave.

—Charles Spurgeon [4]

CONTAGIOUS GENEROSITY

This idea of paying it forward has become a national phenomenon as of late. A Chick-fil-A restaurant in Houston, Texas, experienced a sixty-seven-car chain of customers who paid it forward. The *New York Times* reported the possibility that generosity among strangers can be socially contagious.[5] A Starbucks in St. Petersburg, Florida, experienced a pay-it-forward line of customers that resulted in 378 people paying for the next customer's order. This continued for an eleven-hour run.[6] Sunny Myers, a busy mother of two from Raleigh, North Carolina, had money on a Starbucks card app and decided to buy a couple of people coffee. They in turn paid it forward. She posted it to Instagram and Facebook. The card went viral, and so did the mission. People all over the country donated to the cause by putting money on the card to purchase another stranger's cup of coffee, and Operation Red Cup became a national phenomenon.[7] There is now an international Pay It Forward Day when people all over the world agree to do one to three random acts of kindness in a single day. Why do people participate? Gratitude.

The author of Hebrews teaches us in chapter 13 verse 16 that we are not to "forget to do good and to share" because those sacrifices please God. There is something contagious about generosity, and it often has a ripple effect. Little acts of kindness change things, people, and attitudes. They make people feel loved and valued. You will never regret acts of kindness and generosity. Such acts of kindness are just a simple reminder that God intends good and that we are to be active participants in that good. Every person who chose to pay it forward showed a heart of gratitude for the action, or they would not have paid it forward. Therefore when we are grateful, we are more likely to share whatever we have, and those actions honor God and encourage people.

CHEERFULLY GIVING

"God loves a cheerful giver" (2 Cor. 9:7). Have you ever given and not felt good about it? I doubt it. Giving makes us feel good inside. Giving gives us a sense of well-being, as if we are making a small difference in the lives of others. Therefore our attitude in giving needs to be out of right motives, never out of regret or compulsion. We should give what we have purposed in our heart to give (2 Cor 9:6–7). Also, we should give according to our ability. We know that God will provide our needs according to His riches in glory. Shouldn't we reflect our heavenly Father? Cheerfully give.

In Christian theology the pay-it-forward concept cannot look at God, the giver of the gift, as the one who is being paid back. Instead we pay it forward out of a heart of gratitude to God, not out of indebtedness. Generosity produces thanksgiving to God. It increases the harvest of our own righteousness. You do not pay back because you have a debt that is owed. You pay forward because you have a heart of thanksgiving and you want to graciously share what you have been given.

Shareworthy

If you have much, give your wealth; if you have little, give your heart.
—Anonymous [8]

Paying It Forward

The Word tells us that to whom much is given, much is required (Luke 12:48). We learn through our study of Scripture that there is one who scatters and yet increases all the more, while one holds back what is justly due and the holding back results in *want* (Prov. 11:24). Do you scatter, or do you hold back? Remember that scattering results in increase, while holding back results in want.

The prophet Isaiah discussed generosity and what it can do in our own lives:

> Is not this the fast that I have chosen: to loose the bonds of wickedness, to undo the heavy burdens, and to let the oppressed go free, and break every yoke? Is it not to divide your bread with the hungry and bring the poor who are outcasts into your house? When you see the naked, to cover him and not hide yourself from your own flesh? Then your light shall break forth as the morning, and your healing shall spring forth quickly, and your righteousness shall go before you; the glory of the Lord shall be your reward.
> —Isaiah 58:6–8

During the time of my illness I was walking in our neighborhood with my husband, and the walk required all the strength I could muster. Ken was shocked that I was struggling so desperately. After we came back from our walk and I was resting, I tried to breathe in air for four counts. My lungs were too weak to do so. I went to church the next day and taught my adult Bible fellowship class, and I could not find my words. All I could think was, "God, I know You are able."

From the time God called me into ministry, I have prayed for people to be healed. I've prayed for spiritual healing, physical healing, and emotional healing, believing that God is well able to perform it at any given time. I have had a heart to believe and have utilized my faith on behalf of people who were in desperate need. I believe today I am reaping a harvest from what I have sown praying for healing for others. I've often wondered what would have happened had I not used the gifts I'd been given. That being said, there are many saints of God who have gone on to be with the Lord although they spent a lifetime of prayer on their knees for others. Therein lies a mystery we will not understand until we get to heaven.

In my heart, even through the time fighting illness, I felt that I had much more to give, much more to live for, and much more to pay forward. I know that I have received a bountiful harvest from the Lord. I've been given a second chance in life. His kindness is unmerited, His love endless, and His grace a free gift. Isn't that reason alone to pay it forward? In some small way this book is a way for me to pay it forward. It is a way to give God glory for the second chance I've been given. It's a way that I can pass on the precious lessons learned from a very difficult trial. It is a way to help others be intentional in living a regret-free life now, by living life according to God's perfect plan. Do not wait. Perform those acts of kindness today, paying it forward and living your life free of regret.

INTENTIONAL LIVING

- Be a blessing because you've been given blessings.
- Develop a lifestyle of cheerful, generous giving.
- Share not only your wealth but also your spiritual gifts and talents.
- Share the wisdom and knowledge God has given you.
- Do random acts of kindness, and do it in His name.
- Know that God gives the seed and He multiplies it so as to use it for His glory.
- Expect increase and pay it forward.

CHAPTER 12

IMPACT, INFLUENCE, AND INVEST

Our days are numbered. One of the primary goals in our lives should be to prepare for the day on which our number is up. The legacy we leave is not just in our possessions, but in the quality of our lives. What preparations should we be making now? The greatest waste in all of our earth, which cannot be recycled or reclaimed, is our waste of the time that God has given us each day.

—BILLY GRAHAM[1]

I WOKE UP ONE morning and thoughts flooded my mind: "What am I going to leave behind when my time comes? What have I adequately passed on to my children, and what do I yet have to pass on? What legacy will I leave?" Now I ask you: How will you live your life in such a way that you can say, "I have no regrets"? What will be your life's legacy? This thought comes to mind: before you can leave a legacy, you must first build one and then live one. Three key takeaways for those who want to build a spiritual legacy are summed up in these words: impact, influence, and invest.

Pillar of Abundant Living

Hear, O Israel: The LORD is our God. The LORD is one! And you shall love the LORD your God with all your heart and with all your soul and with all your might. These words, which I am commanding you today, shall be in your heart.

—Deuteronomy 6:4–6

BUILD IT, LIVE IT, LEAVE IT

In the last few months of his life my father was visiting our home in North Carolina and called my family into our den. We gathered around him, and he prayed the most passionate prayer I'd ever heard him pray. By faith he passed on his spiritual legacy. He blessed us with a heartfelt plea to God that we be granted the continuation of his ministry. His heart was already quite enlarged from the damage suffered through heart attacks over the years, and the doctors were now simply trying to keep him as comfortable as possible. He had lost a significant amount of weight and found it a real struggle to walk any distance without becoming fatigued. This day though, God had given him strength. He was filled with the power to pray, and the Spirit of the Lord filled the room. He pronounced a spiritual blessing over our lives and ministry call. I remember thinking to myself at that time, "I want to live up to that blessing."

Billy Graham once said, "The greatest legacy one can pass on to one's children and grandchildren is not money or other material things accumulated in one's life, but rather a legacy of character and faith."[2] I began a journey of searching out how I could become more impactful for the kingdom of God and leave a legacy of character and faith. I wanted to know how I could live a life of influence, and I was determined, as I had seen my own father and mother do, to invest in the lives of others: impact, influence, and invest.

I learned from my father how important it is to leave a spiritual legacy. His deathbed proclamation of having "no regrets" was not born out of his material wealth or his earthly success. Rather, it was based upon the realization that he had done all he could to live for the Lord, introduce his children to Jesus, and lead others to Christ. When my father went home to be with the Lord, we had a viewing the night before his funeral. Oddly enough I did not feel the overwhelming sadness that plagued me right after his death, but instead I felt as though I was at a wedding banquet. I felt such an incredible sense of peace and joy. That may sound strange, but for the entire night all the people he had impacted shared stories of how my father had influenced their lives. I clearly saw the love in their eyes for my dad. I remember one woman said to me, "Robin, I know, without a doubt, had it not been for your father's prayers, I would have been dead." He loved people. He cared about their struggles and helped others whenever and wherever he could. He lived a life of no regrets, and he always modeled for me the importance of sharing the gospel, loving people, and enjoying life to the fullest, even in the small things that seem so insignificant.

It was not until I struggled with severe health issues myself that I began to understand with great clarity the importance of those lessons. We feel as if we will live forever, that we have plenty of time, and that we will get to those important priorities when we retire. But in an instant life as you know it can change dramatically; hence the importance of this message. One of the most important assignments we have is to pass on to the next generation all that we have learned in our life about God, the power of His love, and the depths of His compassion. It is through that understanding that we all become more like Him in our thoughts, actions, and deeds. And it is in that understanding that we begin to make decisions that lead to a life well lived without regrets because we live to serve and please Him. Do you want to leave a spiritual legacy? If so, build it and live it; then you can truly leave behind a life of significance that will impact others for His glory.

Shareworthy

All our pleasures and possessions are consigned to oblivion, but the legacy we leave for Christ will endure forever.

—David Jeremiah[3]

BUILDING A LEGACY

Sir Nicholas Winton left a significant legacy. He single-handedly saved more than 650 Jewish children from the fate of the Holocaust in 1938. England had passed a rule that allowed Jewish refugees under the age of seventeen to come there, provided they had a war-ranty of fifty pounds deposited to demonstrate that they had the capability to return to Czechoslovakia and had a place to stay. When Nicholas heard this, he decided he would help as many youth as pos-sible. In 1988, while sitting in a live show called *That's Life*, the host asked if there was anyone in the audience who had been impacted by Sir Nicholas Winton. Shocked and surprised by the recognition, he slowly turned around and found that he was completely surrounded by the children he had helped survive the Holocaust. He lived to be 106 years old and died in 2015, but the memory of his life well lived continues on today.[4] Now that's impact.

Know God

What will your life say about you after you are gone? Will you be leaving a legacy that will far outlast your short time here on this earth? To begin to build a legacy, pray and ask God for direction. Ask Him what to do and where to start. The only impactful actions that will carry on into eternity will be those that have been led of the Lord. Has God put something in your heart to do already and you've been waiting for a more opportune time? Don't wait. Do it now.

Benjamin Franklin once said, "If you would not be forgotten as soon as you are dead, either write something worth reading or do something worth writing."[5]

Write something worth reading or do something worth writing about; in other words, make an impact. That's good advice. I pon-dered my father's deathbed statement of "I have no regrets" for many years, and I concluded he had no regrets because he made an impact. Then I asked how my father made an impact. He was a pastor for fifty years and established five churches. He was in a gospel quartet group called the Freedom-Aires. He lived a rich, successful life. Still, I was puzzled by his statement that he had no regrets.

I have already had plenty of regrets. I managed an optometric practice for thirteen years after graduating from college, and I made a good income. I had paid vacations to Hilton Head and New York every year, and I had a nice new home that my husband and I had custom built with a beautiful in-ground pool in a wonderful neighborhood. We had a tremendous group of friends who would get together on a weekly basis and have cookouts and neighborhood parties. I had a yuppie (young, upwardly mobile professional) life. Life was good, but it wasn't what God had for me. Then out of the blue God said to me in my time of prayer, "Go home, and know Me!"

Do you know God, or do you just know of Him? In all actuality, living with no regrets all starts with knowing God personally. Though I knew God in that I was saved, I did not have intimacy with Him. I knew what He was saying to me—He wanted me to really know Him. *To know* carries the connotation of intimacy. It suggests being relational and personal. You may know of many people, but you really know your best friends. Building a spiritual legacy starts by getting to know God personally and intimately and following His plans for your life.

We had built our lives as a two-income family. We had plans. But to build a spiritual legacy, we had to follow God's plans and not the plans we devised for ourselves. Giving up my career was certainly not part of my plan. Stop and think: What would you do if God asked you to give up something dear to you? What would you do if He asked you to live on less or be a stay-at-home mom? He may just do it.

Moses knew God. The Lord would speak to Moses face-to-face, as a man speaks with his friend (Exod. 33:11). Paul said he counted "everything as loss for the excellence of the knowledge of Christ Jesus…to know Him, and the power of His resurrection" (Phil. 3:8, 10). Jesus prayed, "This is eternal life: that they may know You, the only true God, and Jesus Christ, whom You have sent" (John 17:3). Do you know Him in a personal and intimate way as you know your very best friend? My father knew God. It is only through intimacy with God that we can truly impact the lives of others. Intimacy with God gives us the boldness and confidence to witness to others as well as the urgency to do so. I think about my father's funeral, and as I said, it was a real home-going. That night as I received our visitors one after another, they hugged me and shared powerful stories of how my father had impacted their lives. One after another I was told how he had prayed for them, encouraged them, helped them out of a bind, comforted them in their time of need, and loved them.

My heart was so filled with joy that even though I stood beside his coffin, I was overwhelmed with love and joy—I had no grief that night, only a celebration of a life well lived. It brings tears to my eyes just thinking about what a beautiful legacy I had been given.

Live a life of character

Friends can be very impactful in our lives. Certain people in our circle of friendship influence our lives greatly. For instance, I went parasailing in Hawaii with a good friend, something my family could never get me to do. I also went on a catamaran, a small sailing vessel, in Key West with that same friend. She said she could sail; she could not. We spent two and a half hours stranded at sea, and then were towed back to the beach. Can you imagine? Friends can impact us for good or get us into trouble. Sometimes it can be a little of both. Proverbs 13:20 says, "He who walks with wise men will be wise, but a companion of fools will be destroyed." Friends can make a huge difference in our lives. We must choose wisely or suffer the consequences of not doing so.

Let's take a look at the biblical story of Ruth and Naomi, who were two very close friends. This story is one of the clearest examples in Scripture of how important it is to impart into the lives of those around us and leave a lasting legacy.

The Book of Ruth is considered to be one of the crown jewels of the Old Testament because it encompasses the mystery of the kingdom of God and within a few short chapters establishes foundational principles of our faith: Jew and Gentile becoming one, salvation, redemption, and the genealogy of Jesus Christ. It was written during the period of the Judges, which was one of the darkest times in the history of Israel. This story starts out as a story of pain, loss, famine, death, and despair, but it quickly becomes a story of protection, provision, redemption, and restoration. The characters portray the depth of loyalty, commitment, and servanthood that should mirror the life and walk of every dedicated believer.

Following is a brief synopsis of the historic account: Naomi was just an ordinary woman who loved God. Naomi moved with her husband and two sons from Bethlehem to Moab because of a famine in the land of Judah. Naomi lost her husband and then later her two sons, both of whom married Moabite women. This left her with Orpah and Ruth, her newly widowed daughters-in-law.

Naomi found herself in unfamiliar and frightening circumstances. Have you ever been there? Have you ever experienced great loss in your life? Have you ever been in a place where you have been left with virtually nothing? I have, and I know how scary that place can be. If you are there right now, turn to the Lord. He will help you in those dark moments of life. Remember, it is in those dark moments when God will give the most treasured messages for you to share with others.

Naomi decided to go back to Judah, and she told her two daughters-in-law, Orpah and Ruth, that they were released from their obligation to care for her. She told them that they should go back home to their people. Orpah returned home, but Ruth clung to Naomi and decided to go forward with her.

We are going to focus primarily on these two women: Ruth and Naomi. Ruth's name means "lovely friend." She was the widow of Naomi's son, Mahlon. Ruth chose to move back to Naomi's land and decided to leave her people because of her loyalty to and love for Naomi. Naomi's name means "pleasant or delightful." This gives us an indication of her persona. Naomi was the widow of Elimelech, meaning "God is King." She was the mother of Chilion, meaning "pining away," and Mahlon, meaning "sick." Both sons died. If you look into Scripture, you will see throughout that there is a principle of the importance of names and how they will often reflect the character of an individual. Naomi was a mentor to Ruth and Orpah. She was a devout Jew of noble character and a woman full of truth and wisdom. These characteristics helped her to build a strong spiritual legacy and to make an impact on Ruth's life.

What characteristics do you feel will result in a rich, spiritual legacy? Take a few minutes and write down what characteristics are most important to you, and then share them with your family, telling them why you feel these characteristics are most important. Your name will live on through your children, and so will your character. How do we gain godly characteristics such as wisdom, truth, and noble character? We choose them. Be known for your kindness. Be constantly growing in wisdom. Be constantly walking in truth. The Bible clearly reads, "Do not let mercy and truth forsake you; bind them around your neck, write them on the tablet of your heart, so you will find favor and good understanding in the sight of God and man" (Prov. 3:3–4).

LIVING A LEGACY

Kindness and truth bring on the favor of God and a good reputation in the sight of God and man. Therefore grow in kindness and truth. If you want to truly live a life of significance and leave a spiritual legacy, learn to walk in a way that will bring the favor of God into your life. Naomi lived what she believed. She walked out her faith. She impacted two pagan girls, and they in turn loved her deeply. Naomi relinquished her daughters-in-law of their responsibility to care for her. Ruth decided to go forward while Orpah decided to go back. Ruth valued Naomi enough to give up what she had known her whole life and move toward something better. Naomi impacted, influenced, and invested in Ruth's life, and they both greatly benefited from the relationship.

Let's look further at this perfect example of a biblical relationship that impacted the world and left a spiritual legacy as we focus on three power words to help you live a legacy worth leaving behind: *impact, influence, invest.* I want these three words to stick in your mind.

Ruth and Naomi were two poor widows who thought they had nothing to give. We will find that Naomi had nothing to give but her wisdom, and Ruth had nothing to give but her loyalty. Through this divine connection the course was set for a dramatically enhanced life and later for a spiritual legacy that would eventually lead to the birth of the Messiah. Naomi was impactful in Ruth's life because she took the time to invest in it and share the truth by which she lived.

Here is my challenge to you. If you are a Naomi, find your Ruth. If you are a Ruth, find your Naomi. What do I mean by that statement? Biblically, older women are to teach younger women. If you have a lot of knowledge and wisdom to pour into someone, then find her and share your wisdom. If you are young in the faith, find someone who is more mature and who is willing to help you navigate your way through life. Relationships matter, and the right relationships can make a world of difference in your life. How would you feel if your life was lived in such a way that those unbelievers in your life—your family, your friends, your neighbors, your coworkers, anyone in your circle of influence—would say, "Because you are who you are, I want to serve your God." The legacy you leave will be imprinted into the hearts of every life you touch. As you pass on all you have learned, others whom you influence will be impacted, thus leaving their own legacy, and the ripples of righteousness are beautifully passed on to another generation.

IMPACT

Our first power word is *impact.* There is no greater impact you can have on an individual than to share the truth of the gospel: the death, burial, and resurrection of Jesus Christ. A woman named Jenny heard that story, the story of the gospel. I was hosting a women's conference in Roxboro, North Carolina, about ten years ago. Jenny attended the conference because a friend invited her to come and purchased a ticket for her. This woman had been addicted to drugs and had prostituted her body to pay for her addiction, but her life was radically changed through the gospel of Christ. Jenny received the truth of God's love, and when she did, she walked away from a life of drug addiction and prostitution to a life of peace, joy, and love. Jenny heard that Jesus loved her enough to die for her. She heard that through faith in Jesus all of her sins would be washed away. She heard that He paid the penalty for her sins so that she would not have to. From that one event, in an instant Jenny would never be the same again, finally freed from the pain of her past. After her deliverance Jenny changed the course of destruction in her life and decided to raise her children in church. Her legacy will be one of faith instead of failure, victory instead of victimization, freedom instead of bondage.

Katherine heard that same story, the gospel. She had attended church, led a moral life, was a philanthropist, and loved life. But at age sixty-three, after attending one of my Bible studies, she realized that Jesus was just in her head, not in her heart. She bowed her head, held my hand, and committed her life to the Lord, forever changed.

Ruth too heard that message of love, grace, and mercy. Naomi told Ruth about her God. Naomi lived her life in front of Ruth in such a way that Ruth wanted what Naomi had. Because of Naomi's example, Ruth responded to her saying, "Your people shall be my people and your God my God" (Ruth 1:16). She essentially said, "Because you are who you are, Naomi, I want to know your God." What did Naomi do that so impacted Ruth? She told Ruth about her one and true God. From their story we can learn that we too can be impactful by sharing the gospel with our friends, family, and coworkers. We learn to be impactful in the way we walk, talk, and love. It was the way Naomi walked, talked, and loved that left such an impact in Ruth's life.

My sweet father lived this. He would be in Walmart, the grocery store, or anywhere else people would listen, and he would ask, "Do you know Jesus?" He would share the good news of the gospel whenever and wherever he could. You too can start now and live a valuable life unto the Lord. You can impact people for the kingdom of God and leave a spiritual legacy that will flow down to your children and your grandchildren.

Shareworthy

If therefore our houses be houses of the Lord, we shall for that reason love home, reckoning our daily devotion the sweetest of our daily delights; and our family-worship the most valuable of our family-comforts....A church in the house will be a good legacy, nay, it will be a good inheritance, to be left to your children after you.

—Matthew Henry[6]

Actions

As you start this journey of living an impactful life, remember that people watch the way you live more than the words you choose to say. Actions speak louder than words, and all of heaven watches. Therefore be impactful by the way you walk: "Whoever says he remains in Him ought to walk as He walked" (1 John 2:6). Do you walk in faith or fear, joy or despair, peace or anxiety? Do you walk in a way that pleases the Lord and honors people?

Words

Scripture also talks of the power of the tongue: "Death and life are in the power of the tongue, and those who love it will eat its fruit" (Prov. 18:21). Be impactful in the way you talk. Be an exhorter, someone who builds up with your words. Refrain from slander or gossip. Your words are very important. Scripture says that by your words you will be either acquitted or condemned (Matt. 12:37). The Word also tells us that we will give an account on the Day of Judgment for every careless word (Matt. 12:36). Words can form and shape the future of a child. They can heal or destroy a marriage. They can build or sever friendships. If we guard our lips, we will preserve our lives, but if we speak harshly, the Bible says we will come to ruin (Prov. 13:3). Be careful with your words; use them to make an impact and live a legacy. Use them to build the kingdom of God.

Have you ever said hurtful things to anyone? I have. Have you ever apologized for those words? I have. It's not an easy thing to do, but our children and grandchildren are watching. So are the Ruths of the world. Be careful with the words you choose, and choose them wisely.

Love

Scripture also says we can make an impact by the way we love: "By this all men will know that you are My disciples, if you have love for one another" (John 13:35).

As Christians we need to show compassion for those who are hurting. We need to help those in need. We need to care for those suffering. Do you care about those less fortunate?

Shareworthy

Our Lord told His disciples that love and obedience were organically united.... The final test of love is obedience.

—A. W. Tozer [7]

Impact those around you

How do you walk, talk, and love? Ask yourself, "Am I walking in a way that would draw others into the kingdom?" Naomi's impact was not just through what she said; it was also the way she lived her life and the love she showed to those around her. My future daughter-in-law calls my home the Jesus house. Now hear me: I do not preach to her, but I live my life in such a way that she, and everyone who knows me, knows where I stand and what I believe. Be impactful by the way you walk, talk, and love. Again, the Ruths of this world are watching.

We learn through the story of Ruth and Naomi that divinely inspired connections greatly enhance your life. Those connections will enrich your life and above all honor God. Therefore find someone and pour your life into them. Again, I challenge you: If you are a Naomi, find your Ruth. If you are a Ruth, find your Naomi. Find someone—your children, your grandchildren, your neighbor, your coworker, someone—and pour your life into them. Winston Churchill said this: "We make a living by what we get, but we make a life by what we give." [8]

Pillar of Abundant Living

Iron sharpens iron, so a man sharpens the countenance of his friend.

—Proverbs 27:17

INFLUENCE

The second power word we are going to look at is *influence*. Ruth was a Moabite, a pagan from a pagan nation. The Moabites served false gods, primarily the god Chemosh. They were God-haters. They sacrificed babies to their gods. They were a people birthed out of Lot's incestuous relationship with his daughter (Gen. 19:36–37). If you look in 2 Kings 3:27, you will find an incident where the king of Moab sacrificed his firstborn son as a burnt offering on the wall of the city so that they would defeat the Israelites, whom they hated. They were a vicious people. However, Naomi did not allow the pagan society of Moab to influence her. No, she influenced the society in which she lived.

Do we allow our culture to influence our thinking? Do we follow cultural mores, or do we follow the written Word of God? The people we surround ourselves with have a great bearing here. Have you surrounded yourself with friends who bring wisdom into your life or those who bring dissension and discord? Have you surrounded yourself with mature believers or babes in the faith?

Naomi understood the culture, and she knew her God. So how can we be influential in our culture? We can look at the life of Naomi. Naomi had a biblical worldview. She did not let the corruption of the society in which she lived affect her relationship with her God. She lived in a way that encouraged those around her to follow God. Therefore, to have real influence, we must have a biblical worldview and stand firmly on it. Having a biblical worldview is paramount to establishing a godly legacy. Standing on a biblical worldview and making every decision based upon the precepts found in Scripture will solidify who you really are in the hearts and minds of those who know you, thereby creating a godly legacy.

Pillar of Abundant Living

Do not be conformed to this world, but be transformed by the renewing of your mind, that you may prove what is the good and acceptable and perfect will of God.

—Romans 12:2

As you decide to live out a strong spiritual legacy and influence those around you, do not be moved by our culture. You cannot think like the world. You cannot accept the ways of the world. You cannot go along with what the world says is good or acceptable. The ways of this world are fleeting and forever changing with no real staying power. The Word, however, is sure. It is solid. It is never changing. The Word tells us that "whatever you do in word or deed, do all in the name of the Lord Jesus, giving thanks to God the Father through Him" (Col 3:17). It tells us not to conform to the evil desires we had when we lived in ignorance, but to be holy because He is holy (1 Pet. 1:14–15).

If you are going to have wisdom to impart to others and to influence your culture, you have to get wisdom for yourself first, so be dedicated to the knowing the Word of God and walking in it. We talked earlier about knowing God—to know God is to know His Word. The only real influence you can have on others that will have lasting, eternal value is the biblical wisdom and knowledge you impart to others. The Bible says, "Your word is a lamp to my feet and a light to my path" (Ps. 119:105). God clearly promises in His Word that He will instruct you, teach you, and counsel you (Ps. 32:8). I desperately need His leadership in my life, and so do you. In knowing the Word of God, you will also grow in knowing God better and better. His Word directs us, instructs us, cleanses us, convicts us, restores us, and comforts us. It is His Word passed on to others that will leave an impact on their lives.

If we are to be influential as we live out a spiritual legacy, then we need to be culturally aware and biblically relevant. The Bible says in the last days it will be as the days of Noah and Lot (Luke 17:26, 28). The days of Noah represent moral corruption, and the days of Lot represent sexual perversion. We live in a biblically illiterate nation in a time of moral corruption and sexual perversion, and now many churches are agreeing with the culture over the clear mandates of the written Word. The Bible says to stand firm or you will not stand at all (Isa. 7:9, niv). It says that we are to come out of this world and be separate (2 Cor. 6:17). It says that we are to differentiate between holy and unholy, clean and unclean (Lev. 10:10).

Naomi knew the culture. Naomi knew the Torah (the first five books of the Bible). She knew her God. For us to be culturally aware and biblically relevant, we must make our judgments based on biblical criteria as Naomi did. We can be a people of truth and minister with truth that does not waver or change. We can maintain cultural integrity and awareness while applying biblical principles across cultures, across generations, and across nationalities. If you have a biblical worldview and are culturally aware, you look and see things from a heavenly perspective. You weigh and measure decisions based on biblical principles. As you strive to know and understand the heart of God, you will then have true influence that will have eternal value.

INVEST

That brings us to our third power word: *invest*. Ruth invested in Naomi. Naomi invested in Ruth. Let me give you the rest of the story. The pair traveled back to Judah, and Ruth gleaned in the field of a distant relative, Boaz, and Naomi instructed her to go to the threshing floor and to lie at his feet. By this ancient custom Ruth was actually asking Boaz to cover her, as in a marriage proposal, to become her husband. He was overwhelmed but agreed to it as long as a man who was a relative closer than he would not marry her. Traditionally the other man would have the first right of refusal. Boaz asked the closer relative and he refused, so Boaz bought their property and took Ruth as his wife. Through that purchase he redeemed Ruth so that her husband's family name would not be cut off. Boaz became the kinsman redeemer. (See Ruth 2–4.) This is a perfect picture of Jesus as He too has bought us with His precious blood, thus paying the debt for our sins so we would not have to.

Out of Ruth's investment of following Naomi, Ruth got a rich, handsome husband, Boaz. Naomi got a step-grandchild she would have never had out of her investment in Ruth's life. Ruth and Naomi got a lifelong friendship, and Ruth and Boaz lived and then left a spiritual legacy that impacts us today. The legacy you leave behind is determined by the decisions you make today. Obed, Ruth's child, was the father of Jesse, and Jesse was the father of King David, and this spiritual legacy led to the birth of Jesus Christ of Nazareth (Matt. 1:4–6).

Pillar of Abundant Living

Thus says the LORD: Let not the wise man glory in his wisdom, and let not the mighty man glory in his might, let not the rich man glory in his riches; but let him who glories glory in this, that he understands and knows Me, that I am the LORD who exercises lovingkindness, justice, and righteousness in the earth. For in these things I delight, says the LORD.

—Jeremiah 9:23-24

LEAVE IT

When I was faced with my own mortality, I realized just how important it is to leave a spiritual legacy. I took a personal inventory to discover how I could improve upon what I had already started to build and live. I was determined in my heart to leave something of value here and to look forward to the rewards I had accumulated on behalf of Christ: souls that I had in some way impacted. There is urgency in my heart even after my illness because now I know firsthand that no man is guaranteed tomorrow. Do not wait. Plan for tomorrow, but live for today.

Do you invest in your own spiritual growth and maturity? Will you consider investing in others? Build your legacy by knowing God and having character. You can know God, not just in a casual way, but intimately and personally. And then live well to pass on a strong spiritual legacy. You can impact others by sharing the gospel. You can influence your culture by having a biblical worldview and being culturally aware and biblically relevant. You can invest in others by becoming a mentor and a godly friend with biblical wisdom to share. Your children and your grandchildren will be impacted by those decisions. They will watch your life, and what you do or do not do will speak volumes to them.

Do you know Him or just know of Him? If you were to die today, do you know for certain that you are going to heaven? You can be certain: "I have written these things to you who believe in the name of the Son of God, that you may know that you have eternal life" (1 John 5:13). Here are the steps to being certain of eternal life:

+ Know salvation is a free gift (Eph. 2:8).
+ Recognize there is none that is righteous (Rom. 3:10–12).
+ Realize we all sin and fall short of the glory of God (Rom. 3:23).
+ Believe in your heart and confess with your mouth that Jesus died, was buried, and arose on the third day (Rom. 10:9).
+ Understand you have been bought with a price (1 Cor. 6:20).
+ Know you have a kinsman redeemer, and His name is Jesus (Gal. 4:4–7; Heb. 2:11, 16–18; 4:14–16).

Leaving a Legacy

What will be your spiritual legacy? Can God use you to further His kingdom? Will you impact the lost by the life you choose to live? Will you be an influencer of those around you? Will you invest in others and allow them to invest in you?

God's plan is perfect. He can take the most messed-up situations, the greatest losses of our lives, the things we see as our greatest failures, and turn them into something beautiful. The story of Naomi's family and the way it has endured is a universal theme that we can all embrace, knowing that God is aware of every detail of our lives. He is working behind the scenes even when we cannot feel His presence. Even Ruth, a pagan and a foreigner from the despised Moabites, could live God's plan toward fulfillment. So can you. Live today without regrets. Embrace every day as a gift from God, and leave a legacy that endures into eternity.

INTENTIONAL LIVING

- Get to know God intimately.
- Choose your friends wisely.
- Learn to share the gospel.
- Walk according to the Word, not according to cultural mores.
- Talk in a way that honors God and honors people.
- Love people in such a way that they crave what you have.
- Take a personal inventory of what you want the world to remember about you, work toward those goals, and leave a spiritual legacy that will follow you into eternity.

THE THIRTY-DAY LOVE CHALLENGE

Fill out this form each day for thirty days to track how well you love those around you. Push to do a little better each day.

Love is patient, love is kind. It does not envy, it does not boast, it is not proud. It does not dishonor others, it is not self-seeking, it is not easily angered, it keeps no record of wrongs. Love does not delight in evil but rejoices with the truth. It always protects, always trusts, always hopes, always perseveres.

—1 Corinthians 13:4–7, niv

Characteristics	Daily Self Rating (1–10)	Why?	What will I do differently tomorrow?
Love is patient.			
Love is kind.			
Love does not envy.			
Love does not boast.			
Love is not proud.			
Love does not dishonor others.			
Love is not self-seeking.			
Love is not easily angered.			
Love keeps no record of wrongs.			
Love does not delight in evil.			
Love rejoices with the truth.			
Love always protects.			
Love always trusts.			
Love always hopes.			
Love always perseveres.			

DAY 01

Characteristics	Daily Self Rating (1–10)	Why?	What will I do differently tomorrow?
Love is patient.			
Love is kind.			
Love does not envy.			
Love does not boast.			
Love is not proud.			
Love does not dishonor others.			
Love is not self-seeking.			
Love is not easily angered.			
Love keeps no record of wrongs.			
Love does not delight in evil.			
Love rejoices with the truth.			
Love always protects.			
Love always trusts.			
Love always hopes.			
Love always perseveres.			

DAY 02

Characteristics	Daily Self Rating (1–10)	Why?	What will I do differently tomorrow?
Love is patient.			
Love is kind.			
Love does not envy.			
Love does not boast.			
Love is not proud.			
Love does not dishonor others.			
Love is not self-seeking.			
Love is not easily angered.			
Love keeps no record of wrongs.			
Love does not delight in evil.			
Love rejoices with the truth.			
Love always protects.			
Love always trusts.			
Love always hopes.			
Love always perseveres.			

DAY 03

Characteristics	Daily Self Rating (1–10)	Why?	What will I do differently tomorrow?
Love is patient.			
Love is kind.			
Love does not envy.			
Love does not boast.			
Love is not proud.			
Love does not dishonor others.			
Love is not self-seeking.			
Love is not easily angered.			
Love keeps no record of wrongs.			
Love does not delight in evil.			
Love rejoices with the truth.			
Love always protects.			
Love always trusts.			
Love always hopes.			
Love always perseveres.			

DAY 04

Characteristics	Daily Self Rating (1–10)	Why?	What will I do differently tomorrow?
Love is patient.			
Love is kind.			
Love does not envy.			
Love does not boast.			
Love is not proud.			
Love does not dishonor others.			
Love is not self-seeking.			
Love is not easily angered.			
Love keeps no record of wrongs.			
Love does not delight in evil.			
Love rejoices with the truth.			
Love always protects.			
Love always trusts.			
Love always hopes.			
Love always perseveres.			

DAY 05

Characteristics	Daily Self Rating (1–10)	Why?	What will I do differently tomorrow?
Love is patient.			
Love is kind.			
Love does not envy.			
Love does not boast.			
Love is not proud.			
Love does not dishonor others.			
Love is not self-seeking.			
Love is not easily angered.			
Love keeps no record of wrongs.			
Love does not delight in evil.			
Love rejoices with the truth.			
Love always protects.			
Love always trusts.			
Love always hopes.			
Love always perseveres.			

DAY 06

Characteristics	Daily Self Rating (1–10)	Why?	What will I do differently tomorrow?
Love is patient.			
Love is kind.			
Love does not envy.			
Love does not boast.			
Love is not proud.			
Love does not dishonor others.			
Love is not self-seeking.			
Love is not easily angered.			
Love keeps no record of wrongs.			
Love does not delight in evil.			
Love rejoices with the truth.			
Love always protects.			
Love always trusts.			
Love always hopes.			
Love always perseveres.			

DAY 07

Characteristics	Daily Self Rating (1–10)	Why?	What will I do differently tomorrow?
Love is patient.			
Love is kind.			
Love does not envy.			
Love does not boast.			
Love is not proud.			
Love does not dishonor others.			
Love is not self-seeking.			
Love is not easily angered.			
Love keeps no record of wrongs.			
Love does not delight in evil.			
Love rejoices with the truth.			
Love always protects.			
Love always trusts.			
Love always hopes.			
Love always perseveres.			

DAY 08

Characteristics	Daily Self Rating (1–10)	Why?	What will I do differently tomorrow?
Love is patient.			
Love is kind.			
Love does not envy.			
Love does not boast.			
Love is not proud.			
Love does not dishonor others.			
Love is not self-seeking.			
Love is not easily angered.			
Love keeps no record of wrongs.			
Love does not delight in evil.			
Love rejoices with the truth.			
Love always protects.			
Love always trusts.			
Love always hopes.			
Love always perseveres.			

DAY 09

Characteristics	Daily Self Rating (1–10)	Why?	What will I do differently tomorrow?
Love is patient.			
Love is kind.			
Love does not envy.			
Love does not boast.			
Love is not proud.			
Love does not dishonor others.			
Love is not self-seeking.			
Love is not easily angered.			
Love keeps no record of wrongs.			
Love does not delight in evil.			
Love rejoices with the truth.			
Love always protects.			
Love always trusts.			
Love always hopes.			
Love always perseveres.			

DAY 10

Characteristics	Daily Self Rating (1–10)	Why?	What will I do differently tomorrow?
Love is patient.			
Love is kind.			
Love does not envy.			
Love does not boast.			
Love is not proud.			
Love does not dishonor others.			
Love is not self-seeking.			
Love is not easily angered.			
Love keeps no record of wrongs.			
Love does not delight in evil.			
Love rejoices with the truth.			
Love always protects.			
Love always trusts.			
Love always hopes.			
Love always perseveres.			

DAY 11

Characteristics	Daily Self Rating (1–10)	Why?	What will I do differently tomorrow?
Love is patient.			
Love is kind.			
Love does not envy.			
Love does not boast.			
Love is not proud.			
Love does not dishonor others.			
Love is not self-seeking.			
Love is not easily angered.			
Love keeps no record of wrongs.			
Love does not delight in evil.			
Love rejoices with the truth.			
Love always protects.			
Love always trusts.			
Love always hopes.			
Love always perseveres.			

DAY 12

Characteristics	Daily Self Rating (1–10)	Why?	What will I do differently tomorrow?
Love is patient.			
Love is kind.			
Love does not envy.			
Love does not boast.			
Love is not proud.			
Love does not dishonor others.			
Love is not self-seeking.			
Love is not easily angered.			
Love keeps no record of wrongs.			
Love does not delight in evil.			
Love rejoices with the truth.			
Love always protects.			
Love always trusts.			
Love always hopes.			
Love always perseveres.			

DAY 13

Characteristics	Daily Self Rating (1–10)	Why?	What will I do differently tomorrow?
Love is patient.			
Love is kind.			
Love does not envy.			
Love does not boast.			
Love is not proud.			
Love does not dishonor others.			
Love is not self-seeking.			
Love is not easily angered.			
Love keeps no record of wrongs.			
Love does not delight in evil.			
Love rejoices with the truth.			
Love always protects.			
Love always trusts.			
Love always hopes.			
Love always perseveres.			

DAY 14

Characteristics	Daily Self Rating (1–10)	Why?	What will I do differently tomorrow?
Love is patient.			
Love is kind.			
Love does not envy.			
Love does not boast.			
Love is not proud.			
Love does not dishonor others.			
Love is not self-seeking.			
Love is not easily angered.			
Love keeps no record of wrongs.			
Love does not delight in evil.			
Love rejoices with the truth.			
Love always protects.			
Love always trusts.			
Love always hopes.			
Love always perseveres.			

DAY 15

Characteristics	Daily Self Rating (1–10)	Why?	What will I do differently tomorrow?
Love is patient.			
Love is kind.			
Love does not envy.			
Love does not boast.			
Love is not proud.			
Love does not dishonor others.			
Love is not self-seeking.			
Love is not easily angered.			
Love keeps no record of wrongs.			
Love does not delight in evil.			
Love rejoices with the truth.			
Love always protects.			
Love always trusts.			
Love always hopes.			
Love always perseveres.			

DAY 16

Characteristics	Daily Self Rating (1–10)	Why?	What will I do differently tomorrow?
Love is patient.			
Love is kind.			
Love does not envy.			
Love does not boast.			
Love is not proud.			
Love does not dishonor others.			
Love is not self-seeking.			
Love is not easily angered.			
Love keeps no record of wrongs.			
Love does not delight in evil.			
Love rejoices with the truth.			
Love always protects.			
Love always trusts.			
Love always hopes.			
Love always perseveres.			

DAY 17

Characteristics	Daily Self Rating (1–10)	Why?	What will I do differently tomorrow?
Love is patient.			
Love is kind.			
Love does not envy.			
Love does not boast.			
Love is not proud.			
Love does not dishonor others.			
Love is not self-seeking.			
Love is not easily angered.			
Love keeps no record of wrongs.			
Love does not delight in evil.			
Love rejoices with the truth.			
Love always protects.			
Love always trusts.			
Love always hopes.			
Love always perseveres.			

DAY 18

Characteristics	Daily Self Rating (1–10)	Why?	What will I do differently tomorrow?
Love is patient.			
Love is kind.			
Love does not envy.			
Love does not boast.			
Love is not proud.			
Love does not dishonor others.			
Love is not self-seeking.			
Love is not easily angered.			
Love keeps no record of wrongs.			
Love does not delight in evil.			
Love rejoices with the truth.			
Love always protects.			
Love always trusts.			
Love always hopes.			
Love always perseveres.			

DAY 19

Characteristics	Daily Self Rating (1–10)	Why?	What will I do differently tomorrow?
Love is patient.			
Love is kind.			
Love does not envy.			
Love does not boast.			
Love is not proud.			
Love does not dishonor others.			
Love is not self-seeking.			
Love is not easily angered.			
Love keeps no record of wrongs.			
Love does not delight in evil.			
Love rejoices with the truth.			
Love always protects.			
Love always trusts.			
Love always hopes.			
Love always perseveres.			

DAY 20

Characteristics	Daily Self Rating (1–10)	Why?	What will I do differently tomorrow?
Love is patient.			
Love is kind.			
Love does not envy.			
Love does not boast.			
Love is not proud.			
Love does not dishonor others.			
Love is not self-seeking.			
Love is not easily angered.			
Love keeps no record of wrongs.			
Love does not delight in evil.			
Love rejoices with the truth.			
Love always protects.			
Love always trusts.			
Love always hopes.			
Love always perseveres.			

DAY 21

Characteristics	Daily Self Rating (1–10)	Why?	What will I do differently tomorrow?
Love is patient.			
Love is kind.			
Love does not envy.			
Love does not boast.			
Love is not proud.			
Love does not dishonor others.			
Love is not self-seeking.			
Love is not easily angered.			
Love keeps no record of wrongs.			
Love does not delight in evil.			
Love rejoices with the truth.			
Love always protects.			
Love always trusts.			
Love always hopes.			
Love always perseveres.			

DAY 22

Characteristics	Daily Self Rating (1–10)	Why?	What will I do differently tomorrow?
Love is patient.			
Love is kind.			
Love does not envy.			
Love does not boast.			
Love is not proud.			
Love does not dishonor others.			
Love is not self-seeking.			
Love is not easily angered.			
Love keeps no record of wrongs.			
Love does not delight in evil.			
Love rejoices with the truth.			
Love always protects.			
Love always trusts.			
Love always hopes.			
Love always perseveres.			

DAY 23

Characteristics	Daily Self Rating (1–10)	Why?	What will I do differently tomorrow?
Love is patient.			
Love is kind.			
Love does not envy.			
Love does not boast.			
Love is not proud.			
Love does not dishonor others.			
Love is not self-seeking.			
Love is not easily angered.			
Love keeps no record of wrongs.			
Love does not delight in evil.			
Love rejoices with the truth.			
Love always protects.			
Love always trusts.			
Love always hopes.			
Love always perseveres.			

DAY 24

Characteristics	Daily Self Rating (1–10)	Why?	What will I do differently tomorrow?
Love is patient.			
Love is kind.			
Love does not envy.			
Love does not boast.			
Love is not proud.			
Love does not dishonor others.			
Love is not self-seeking.			
Love is not easily angered.			
Love keeps no record of wrongs.			
Love does not delight in evil.			
Love rejoices with the truth.			
Love always protects.			
Love always trusts.			
Love always hopes.			
Love always perseveres.			

DAY 25

Characteristics	Daily Self Rating (1–10)	Why?	What will I do differently tomorrow?
Love is patient.			
Love is kind.			
Love does not envy.			
Love does not boast.			
Love is not proud.			
Love does not dishonor others.			
Love is not self-seeking.			
Love is not easily angered.			
Love keeps no record of wrongs.			
Love does not delight in evil.			
Love rejoices with the truth.			
Love always protects.			
Love always trusts.			
Love always hopes.			
Love always perseveres.			

DAY 26

Characteristics	Daily Self Rating (1–10)	Why?	What will I do differently tomorrow?
Love is patient.			
Love is kind.			
Love does not envy.			
Love does not boast.			
Love is not proud.			
Love does not dishonor others.			
Love is not self-seeking.			
Love is not easily angered.			
Love keeps no record of wrongs.			
Love does not delight in evil.			
Love rejoices with the truth.			
Love always protects.			
Love always trusts.			
Love always hopes.			
Love always perseveres.			

DAY 27

Characteristics	Daily Self Rating (1–10)	Why?	What will I do differently tomorrow?
Love is patient.			
Love is kind.			
Love does not envy.			
Love does not boast.			
Love is not proud.			
Love does not dishonor others.			
Love is not self-seeking.			
Love is not easily angered.			
Love keeps no record of wrongs.			
Love does not delight in evil.			
Love rejoices with the truth.			
Love always protects.			
Love always trusts.			
Love always hopes.			
Love always perseveres.			

DAY 28

Characteristics	Daily Self Rating (1–10)	Why?	What will I do differently tomorrow?
Love is patient.			
Love is kind.			
Love does not envy.			
Love does not boast.			
Love is not proud.			
Love does not dishonor others.			
Love is not self-seeking.			
Love is not easily angered.			
Love keeps no record of wrongs.			
Love does not delight in evil.			
Love rejoices with the truth.			
Love always protects.			
Love always trusts.			
Love always hopes.			
Love always perseveres.			

DAY 29

Characteristics	Daily Self Rating (1–10)	Why?	What will I do differently tomorrow?
Love is patient.			
Love is kind.			
Love does not envy.			
Love does not boast.			
Love is not proud.			
Love does not dishonor others.			
Love is not self-seeking.			
Love is not easily angered.			
Love keeps no record of wrongs.			
Love does not delight in evil.			
Love rejoices with the truth.			
Love always protects.			
Love always trusts.			
Love always hopes.			
Love always perseveres.			

DAY 30

NOTES

FOREWORD

1. Charlie D. Tillman and M. E. Abbey, "Life's Railway to Heaven." Public domain.

CHAPTER 1: LIVE LIKE YOU WERE DYING

1. A. W. Tozer, *The Pursuit of God* (N.p.: Wyatt North, 2013).

2. Charles R. Swindoll, *Man to Man* (Grand Rapids, MI: Zondervan, 1996), 89.

3. "Thomas Ken," AZ Quotes, accessed January 11, 2017, http://www.azquotes.com/quote/1264909.

4. "Warren W. Wiersbe," AZ Quotes, accessed January 11, 2017, http://www.azquotes.com/quote/662719?ref=rear-view-mirror.

CHAPTER 2: TESTS AND MEASUREMENTS

1. A. W. Tozer, *Preparing for Jesus' Return: Daily Live the Blessed Hope* (Bloomington, MN: Bethany House Publishers, 2012).

2. "To Justify the Ways of God to Men," Literary Devices, accessed January 10, 2017, http://literarydevices.net/to-justify-the-ways-of-god-to-men/.

3. Oswald Chambers, *My Utmost for His Highest* (Nashville: Discovery House Publishers, 1992).

4. George Whitefield, *Sermons of George Whitefield* (Peabody, MA: Hendrickson Publishers, 2009), 68.

5. Helen Keller, *The World I Live in and Optimism: A Collection of Essays* (Mineola, NY: Dover Publications, Inc., 2010), 93.

6. Fredrick W. Robertson, "Man's Greatness and God's Greatness" (sermon, June 20, 1852), accessed March 22, 2017, http://www.fwrobertson.com/sermons/ser61.htm.

CHAPTER 3: REFINEMENT: A TEST AND PURIFICATION OF THE HEART

1. "George MacDonald Quotes," accessed November 30, 2016, https://www.goodreads.com/quotes/tag/refinement.

2. A. W. Tozer, *Tozer on Worship and Entertainment* (Camp Hill, PA: Wing Spread Publishers, 1997).

3. Charles Haddon Spurgeon, *Devotional Classics of C. H. Spurgeon* (Lafayette, IN: Sovereign Grace Publishers, 1990).

4. "A. W. Tozer Quotes," Goodreads, accessed January 11, 2017, http://www.goodreads.com/quotes/329596-a-man-by-his-sin-may-waste-himself-which-is.

5. C. H. Spurgeon, "Mercy's Master Motive" (sermon, Metropolitan Tabernacle, Newington, UK, March 17, 1872), accessed November 30, 2016, http://biblehub.com/library/spurgeon/spurgeons_sermons_volume_18_1872/mercys_master_motive.htm.

CHAPTER 4: THE POWER OF PRAYER

1. Charles Spurgeon, *The Treasury of David: Containing an Original Exposition of the Book of Psalms*, Volume I (London: Passmore and Alabaster, 1870).

2. "John Wesley," Goodreads, accessed December 5, 2016, https://www.goodreads.com/author/quotes/151350.John_Wesley?page=2.

3. John Wesley, *Renew My Heart*, compiled by Alice Russie (Uhrichsville, OH: Barbour Publishing, 2011).

4. E. M. Bounds, "Needed—Men and Women of Prayer," The Epworth Era, Volume 25, September 1918, p. 12.

5. E. M. Bounds, *The Complete Works of E.M. Bounds on Prayer: Experience the Wonders of God Through Prayer* (Grand Rapids, MI: Baker Books, 2004).

6. Thomas Watson, *Discourses on Important and Interesting Subjects*, volume 2 (Glasgow: Blackie, Fullarton, & Co., 1829), 112.

7. E. M. Bounds, *The Possibility of Prayer* (N.p.: Start Publishing, 2012).

CHAPTER 5: AUTHENTIC LOVE

1. Philip Yancey, *What's So Amazing About Grace?* (Grand Rapids, MI: Zondervan, 1997), 280.

2. Julian of Norwich, as quoted in Bill Tell, *Lay It Down: Living in the Freedom of the Gospel* (Colorado Springs, CO: NavPress, 2015), 95.

3. Alice G. Walton, "New Study Links Facebook to Depression: But Now We Actually Understand Why," *Forbes*, April 8, 2015, accessed December 5, 2016, http://www.forbes.com/sites/alicegwalton/2015/04/08/new-study-links-facebook-to-depression-but-now-we-actually-understand-why/#6020add72e65.

4. "150 Andrew Murray Quotes," Christian Quotes, accessed January 11, 2017, http://www.christianquotes.info/quotes-by-author/andrew-murray-quotes/#axzz4VTmSjokN.

CHAPTER 6: CHARACTER COUNTS

1. "71 A. W. Tozer Quotes," Christian Quotes, accessed December 6, 2016, http://www.christianquotes.info/quotes-by-author/a-w-tozer-quotes/#ixzz48lLbEgi7.

2. "71 A. W. Tozer Quotes," Christian Quotes, accessed December 6, 2016, http://www.christianquotes.info/quotes-by-author/a-w-tozer-quotes/#ixzz48lM5XDUE.

3. "Character Quotes," Brainy Quote, accessed December 7, 2016, http://www.brainyquote.com/quotes/keywords/character.html.

4. "Charles Spurgeon Quotes," Brainy Quote, accessed December 8, 2016, https://www.brainyquote.com/quotes/quotes/c/charlesspu106282.html.

5. Oswald Chambers, *Biblical Psychology: Christ-Centered Solutions for Daily Problems* (Grand Rapids, MI: Discovery House, 2014).

Chapter 7: Abundant Joy

1. Mother Teresa, *My Life for the Poor* (New York: Ballantine Books, 1987).

2. "Thunderstorms," Florida Disaster, updated January 4, 2012, accessed January 10, 2017, http://www.floridadisaster.org/kids/thunderstorms.htm.

3. Merrill F. Unger, *New Unger's Bible Dictionary* (Chicago: Moody Press, 1988), s.v. "joy."

4. "18 Wonderful Quotes About Joy," Christian Quotes, accessed December 9, 2016, http://www.christianquotes.info/top-quotes/18-wonderful-quotes-about-joy/#ixzz48wVSRvqK.

Chapter 8: Forgive and Forget

1. Henry Ward Beecher, *Life Thoughts, Gathered From the Extemporaneous Discourses of Henry Ward Beecher* (Boston: Phillips, Sampson and Company, 1858), 108.

2. Oswald Chambers, *My Utmost for His Highest* (Grand Rapids, MI: Discovery House Publishers, 2005).

3. "Warren W. Wiersbe," AZ Quotes, accessed January 11, 2017, http://www.azquotes.com/quote/523163?ref=forgiveness.

4. "Forgiveness: Your Health Depends on It," Johns Hopkins Medicine, accessed December 12, 2016, http://www.hopkinsmedicine.org/health/healthy_aging/healthy_connections/forgiveness-your-health-depends-on-it.

5. BibleHub.com, "859. *aphesis*," accessed January 17, 2017, http://biblehub.com/greek/859.htm.

6. *Merriam-Webster Online*, s.v. "as," accessed January 10, 2017, https://www.merriam-webster.com/dictionary/as.

7. "Corrie Ten Boom Quotes," Brainy Quote, accessed December 12, 2016, http://www.brainyquote.com/quotes/quotes/c/corrietenb381187.html.

Chapter 9: Faith Fuel

1. E. M. Bounds, *E. M. Bounds on Prayer* (Peabody, MA: Hendrickson Publishers, 2006), 139.

2. Charles Spurgeon, "False Justification and True" (sermon, Metropolitan Tabernacle, Newington, UK, October 15, 1876), accessed March 22, 2017, http://spurgeongems.org/vols49-51/chs2932.pdf.

3. "Aiden Wilson Tozer Quotes," AZ Quotes, accessed January 11, 2017, http://www.azquotes.com/author/14750-Aiden_Wilson_Tozer.

Chapter 10: Second Chances

1. Oswald Chambers, "The Discipline of Heeding," *My Utmost for His Highest*, February 14, 2017, accessed January 17, 2017, https://utmost.org/classic /the-discipline-of-heeding-classic/.

2. Casey Harper, "Innocent Man Wrongly Jailed For 39 Years Becomes Cleveland's Newest Millionaire," *Daily Caller*, March 20, 2015, accessed December 13, 2016, http://dailycaller.com/2015/03/20/innocent-man -wrongly-jailed-for-39-years-becomes-clevelands-newest-millionaire-video /#ixzz4988Wjh4p.

3. Oswald Chambers, *Conformed to His Image/The Servant as His Lord*, accessed March 23, 2017, https://books.google.com/books?id=8bWWCgAAQB AJ&source=gbs_navlinks_s.

4. "Greg Laurie," AZ Quotes, accessed January 11, 2017, http://www .azquotes.com/quote/725670?ref=wrong-direction.

5. Peter Scazzero, *Old Testament Characters* (Downers Grove, IL: InterVarsity Press, 2000).

6. *Matthew Poole's Commentary*, Jonah 1:2, accessed January 11, 2017, http://biblehub.com/commentaries/poole/jonah/1.htm.

7. Bible Study Tools, "Meno," accessed January 18, 2017, http://www .biblestudytools.com/lexicons/greek/nas/meno.html.

8. "Joseph Franklin Rutherford," AZ Quotes, accessed January 11, 2017, http://www.azquotes.com/quote/901105.

9. Charles Haddon Spurgeon, *Devotional Classics of C. H. Spurgeon* (Lafayette, IN: Sovereign Grace Publishers, Inc., 1990).

Chapter 11: Paying It Forward

1. "John Wesley Quotes," Goodreads, accessed December 15, 2016, https:// www.goodreads.com/author/quotes/151350.John_Wesley.

2. "Warren W. Wiersbe," AZ Quotes, accessed January 11, 2017, http://www .azquotes.com/quote/400336.

3. "Billy Graham Quotes," BrainyQuote, accessed December 15, 2016, https://www.brainyquote.com/quotes/quotes/b/billygraha589700.html.

4. "Charles Spurgeon," AZ Quotes, accessed January 11, 2017, http://www .azquotes.com/quote/609654.

5. Milena Tsvetkova and Michael Macy, "The Science of 'Paying It Forward,'" *New York Times*, March 14, 2014, accessed December 15, 2016, http://www .nytimes.com/2014/03/16/opinion/sunday/the-science-of-paying-it-forward .html?_r=0.

6. Paulina Firozi, "378 People 'Pay It Forward' at Starbucks," *USA Today*, August 21, 2014, accessed December 15, 2016, http://www.usatoday.com

/story/news/nation-now/2014/08/21/378-people-pay-it-forward-at-fla
-starbucks/14380109/.

7. Anna Laurel, "Free Starbucks Coffee Idea Goes Viral," ABC 11 Eyewitness News, November 8, 2013, accessed January 11, 2017, http://abc11.com
/archive/9318665/.

8. "Inspiring Quotes," Pay it Forward Day, accessed December 15, 2016,
http://payitforwardday.com/inspire-me/inspiring-quotes/.

Chapter 12: Impact, Influence, and Invest

1. Billy Graham, *Hope for the Troubled Heart* (Nashville, TN; Thomas
Nelson, 2011).

2. "Billy Graham Quotes," Brainy Quote, accessed December 16, 2016,
https://www.brainyquote.com/quotes/quotes/b/billygraha626354.html.

3. "David Jeremiah," AZ Quotes, accessed January 11, 2017, http://www
.azquotes.com/quote/961687.

4. "Holocaust 'Hero' Sir Nicholas Winton Dies Aged 106," BBC, July 1, 2015,
accessed December 16, 2016, http://www.bbc.com/news/uk-england-33350880;
"Nicholas Winton and the Rescue of Children from Czechoslovakia, 1938–1939,"
Holocaust Encyclopedia, accessed December 16, 2016, https://www.ushmm.org
/wlc/en/article.php?ModuleId=10007780; "60 Minutes: Sir Nicholas Winton
'Saving the Children,'" YouTube video, accessed December 16, 2016, https://
www.youtube.com/watch?v=c0aoifNziKQ.

5. John W. Richardson, "Top 10 Quotes About Leaving a Legacy," Personal
Success Today, April 16, 2013, accessed December 16, 2016, http://
personalsuccesstoday.com/top-10-quotes-about-leaving-a-legacy/.

6. "Matthew Henry," AZ Quotes, accessed January 11, 2017, http://www
.azquotes.com/quote/860116.

7. A. W. Tozer, *That Incredible Christian: How Heaven's Children Live on
Earth* (Camp Hill, PA: Wing Spread Publishers, 1964).

8. "Winston Churchill Quotes," BrainyQuote, accessed December 6, 2016,
http://www.brainyquote.com/quotes/quotes/w/winstonchu131192.html.

ABOUT THE AUTHOR

Robin Bertram Ministries
HEALING HEARTS, TRANSFORMING LIVES

Speaker, Author, Executive Producer of
Freedom Today Television,
National Director of Regions Christian
Women in Media

A UTHOR, SEASONED CONFERENCE speaker, and former host of the nationally syndicated television program *Freedom Today*, Robin Bertram brings a wealth of knowledge and experience to women's platforms across the country. Robin's passion for the Word, love for people, and heart to serve were developed early on in life as a PK and continued through her life's journey. She is a keynote speaker at women's conferences across the country. Her straightforward approach with in-depth biblical insight is healing hearts and transforming lives as she delivers vibrant messages of encouragement, freedom, and victory in Jesus Christ. Robin would love to schedule an event for your church or women's group, and she can be reached directly on her website, on Facebook, or by e-mail at robin@robinbertram.org.

Robin is the vice president of Christian Women in Media and serves on their national advisory board. In addition to *No Regrets*, Robin has authored numerous Bible studies (many of which are available as free downloads on her website) in addition to her first book, *Shadows Among Us*, a comprehensive guide to prayer ministry. Impacting, influencing, investing in women, her mission and message are simple: to spread the gospel to a lost and dying world.

CONNECT WITH ROBIN

Facebook: @officialRobinBertram

Twitter: @RobinBertram

Instagram: @RobinBertram

Pinterest: /robinbertram2

LinkedIn: /in/RobinBertram

Website: www.robinbertram.tv

CONNECT WITH US!

CHARISMA HOUSE

(Spiritual Growth)

f Facebook.com/CharismaHouse

🐦 @CharismaHouse

📷 Instagram.com/CharismaHouse

SILOAM

(Health)

📌 Pinterest.com/CharismaHouse

MODERN ENGLISH VERSION

(Bible)

www.mevbible.com